A Faith Worth Living

A Faith Worth Living

The Dynamics of an Inclusive Gospel

CHUCK QUEEN

RESOURCE *Publications* • Eugene, Oregon

A FAITH WORTH LIVING
The Dynamics of an Inclusive Gospel

Copyright © 2011 Chuck Queen. All rights reserved. Except for brief quotations in critical publications or reviews, no part of this book may be reproduced in any manner without prior written permission from the publisher. Write: Permissions, Wipf and Stock Publishers, 199 W. 8th Ave., Suite 3, Eugene, OR 97401.

Resource Publications
An Imprint of Wipf and Stock Publishers
199 W. 8th Ave., Suite 3
Eugene, OR 97401
www.wipfandstock.com

ISBN 13: 978-1-61097-187-4

Manufactured in the U.S.A.

All scripture quotations contained herein, unless otherwise indicated, are from the New Revised Standard Version Bible, copyright © 1989, by the Division of Christian Education of the National Council of the Churches of Christ in the U.S.A., and are used by permission. All rights reserved.

*To my parents,
Edgar and Phyllis Queen,
whose loving and caring nurture
provided a safe environment to grow a healthy faith,
and to Daniel and Hollie Griffith,
my son-in-law and daughter,
whose parental nurturing
reflects the grace and goodness of the all compassionate God
who is the Father and Mother of us all.*

Contents

Introduction ix

1. Finding Our Center 1
2. God's Dream for the World 28
3. The Triumph of Love 77
4. Living the Faith 118

Bibliography 153

Introduction

WHY BECOME A CHRISTIAN today? With elitism, nationalism, and militarism permeating so much of Christendom, and with so many exclusivistic, dogmatic, egotistical versions of the gospel, it is no wonder that Christianity has such little appeal today among thinking, caring, and globally-minded people.

A Faith Worth Living draws upon the dynamics of a transformative faith, kingdom theology, Jesus' nonviolent atonement, universal salvation, and a radical discipleship to present the theological components and the practical dynamics of a holistic, Christ-centered, inclusive gospel for everyday Christians and spiritual seekers. It weaves together observations and explanations based on scriptural interpretation, theological reflection, and contemporary life experience drawn from film, literature, and our common humanity. This book seeks to integrate an inclusive gospel that is grounded in and pervaded by a theology of God's unconditional love, with the challenges of actualizing this gospel in the daily grind of life.

In a previous book, *The Good News According to Jesus: A New Kind of Christianity for a New Kind of Christian*, my focus centered on the message of Jesus in the Synoptic Gospels (Matthew, Mark, and Luke). In *A Faith Worth Living*, I draw upon other New Testament documents in addition to the Synoptic Gospels, especially the writings of Paul and the Gospel of John, demonstrating that while there are certainly significant differences in theological perspective, the overarching vision conveyed in these writings is consistent with Jesus' vision of the kingdom of God presented in the Synoptic Gospels.

In chapter 1 (Finding Our Center), I engage in a theological and practical exposition of the nature of transformative faith. I distinguish between faith as a set of beliefs and faith as a living reality—the dynamic trust and confidence that connects disciples to the living Christ, the Divine Center out of which disciples of Jesus live. I argue that what we believe is important to the degree that it determines and shapes how we live.

In chapter 2 (God's Dream for the World), I present a vision of human flourishing and societal well-being based on Jesus' vision of God's design for all of human life and creation (the kingdom of God). I offer a glimpse of what a just, compassionate world renewed and reconciled to God, one another, and all creation might look like, sharing some practical insights in the implementation and realization of that vision. I draw upon the theology of Paul to portray the church as an "in Christ" community empowered by the Spirit, serving as an outpost for God's new world.

In chapter 3 (The Triumph of Love), I explain how the death and resurrection of Jesus can be seen as the ultimate demonstration of God's love for humanity and how the salvific event of Christ's life, death, and resurrection can transform human relationships, communities, and individuals. I point out the inconsistencies that occur in traditional Christianity when Paul's metaphors of sacrifice and salvation are interpreted too literally. I introduce an inclusive vision of the cosmic Christ, in whom and through whom all things will be brought together and made whole. I then discuss how Christians, with an inclusive vision of a reconciled universe in Christ, might engage in mutual dialogue with those of other religious faiths who do not share this vision.

In chapter 4 (Living the Faith), I focus on the daily, practical life that disciples of Jesus are called to live in light of God's inclusive, unconditional love. I argue that the invitation to discipleship is an invitation to participate in God's kingdom in the world. While pain and suffering are an unavoidable and inevitable part of the disciple's experience, I contend that discipleship to Jesus is the way to an abundant life. I delineate in some detail the disciple's connection to the world. Disciples experience conflict with the world while engaging in a vital mission and ministry to the world. I conclude by showing that following Jesus calls for faithful endurance and fellowship in Jesus' suffering love.

For too long Christians have been offering the world a gospel that purports to be good news, but when subjected to careful scrutiny and reflection, is exposed as narrow, exclusive, elitist, and condemnatory. It is time to share with the world good news that is authentically good news, a message that inspires faith, nourishes hope, and is immersed in love.

All who participate in this conversation must do so with humility. No one has all the truth. Even if it was possible to possess all the truth, we would still be limited by our capacity to see and grasp it. We all live with contradictions and fall short of living God's dream for the world. We all struggle with the desires and ambitions of our egos, regardless of how good and noble are our theological visions. We do, however, tend to order our lives (or at least we strive to order our lives) according to what we actually believe in our hearts about ultimate reality. It is my hope that this book will provide Christians, students of religion, and spiritual seekers with a lucid vision of the gospel that is inclusive, holistic, and transformative.

Dualistic theology comes in many forms, expressions, and religious traditions. It has been part of the Christian tradition from its beginning. In whatever form it is expressed, it ultimately separates and divides humanity into "us" and "them" (pure/impure, saved/lost, righteous/wicked, etc.), and the division is often based on very simplistic, superficial beliefs and perceptions. In a dualistic system, the mission of the church is mainly one of converting those on the "outside" to the faith of those on the "inside." One problem with dualistic theologies is that they tend to make absolute that which is relative. Good and evil run through every human heart and the decisions that determine whether a person engages in good or evil are very complex, influenced by many factors.

We must articulate more credible explanations of faith. This starts with a healthy, holistic, life-enhancing worldview. Our global future depends upon our willingness to own our past mistakes, rather than duplicate them, and on our capacity to grow up spiritually, emotionally, relationally, socially, and theologically. For people of faith, our theological vision of God and the world forms the foundation for our worldview. A worldview is not an ivory-tower philosophy; rather, it is the foundation on which we construct our lives. It is my contention that a worldview derived from an inclusive gospel, as presented in the following pages, provides rich soil for individuals, communities, and societies to flourish and thrive.

In his beautiful exposition of love in 1 Corinthian 13, Paul wrote, "When I was a child, I spoke like a child, I thought like a child, I reasoned like a child; when I became an adult, I put an end to childish ways" (13:11). It's time for us to put away our childish, dualistic theologies and grow up—to embrace a faith worth living.

1

Finding Our Center

GOD IS CERTAINLY "MORE" than we can begin to imagine. I particularly like Luke's depiction of God in his presentation of Paul's proclamation of the gospel to the philosophers of Athens in the book of Acts. Paul doesn't begin by referencing the Hebrew Scriptures as he so often does with Jews and Hellenists; rather, he begins with an inscription from a Greek object of worship that read, "To an unknown god." Paul links this unknown god to the God who created heaven and earth. This God, says Paul, "does not live in shrines made by human hands, nor is served by human hands, as though he needed anything, since he gives to all mortals life and breath and all things" (Acts 17:24–25). In other words, the God who created all things is self-sufficient and is the source of all human and natural life. The Creator, says Paul, is not far from anyone, because "in him we live and move and have our being" (Acts 17:28). God is the very energy, spirit, or life-force that animates human life.

All God language is symbolic, metaphorical language, because the reality of God (the Transcendent, the Real, the Divine, etc.) cannot be fully captured by our concepts and ideas. It is common for theologians to describe God as both transcendent and immanent; that God, on the one hand, is beyond or more than the reality/substance that constitutes our physical/material and spiritual/immaterial universe, and on the other hand, God is with and in this universe as the very life force that holds it all together, the energy that is in and around the smallest building blocks and particles (quarks?) of creation.

We who are Christians interpret our experience of God in light of the Hebrew-Christian Scriptures. So whatever we may say about God, or however we may conceive of God (and what we have said and conceived run the spectrum from the truly sublime and beautiful to the ridiculously silly and ugly) most of us within this tradition regard God as a personal God. In the Hebrew-Christian tradition, God may be viewed as transpersonal, or more than personal, but God is at least conceived of as personal, manifesting human qualities and characteristics in God's relationship with humans. Jesus scholar and popular Christian theologian, Marcus Borg contends, "Whatever God is ultimately like, our relationship to God is personal. This relationship engages us as persons at our deepest and most passionate level."[1] We experience God more as a presence than as a force; God is encountered as a "you" rather than as an "it." We see this especially in the covenant theology of the Jewish and Christian traditions that conveys "an intrinsically relational model of reality."[2] Without question, in the biblical stories human beings encounter God in a personal way. God is experienced as a Divine Person. God, I have no doubt, is "more than" this, but God is "at least" this.

It is my contention that the foundational reality that we call God, the Divine Reality that is both within and beyond the physical/spiritual universe as we know it, can best be understood as Love. The First Epistle of John has much to say about the importance and necessity of love, making this startling declaration, "God is love, and those who abide in love abide in God, and God abides in them" (1 John 4:16). In Paul's first letter to the Corinthians, he calls upon a divided, fragmented, ego-driven congregation to adopt "the more excellent way" of love. He writes,

> If I speak in the tongues of mortals and of angels, but do not have love, I am a noisy gong or a clanging cymbal. And if I have prophetic powers, and understand all mysteries and all knowledge, and if I have all faith, so as to remove mountains, but do not have love, I am nothing. If I give away all my possessions, and if I hand over my body so that I may boast, but do not have love, I gain nothing... And now faith, hope, and love abide, these three; and the greatest of these is love. 1 Cor 13:1–3, 13

Paul instructs the Colossian Christians, "Above all, clothe yourselves with love, which binds everything together in perfect harmony" (Col 3:14). When Jesus was asked about the greatest commandment, he declared that God's expectation for humanity is grounded in love for God and love for neighbor (Matt 22:34–40).

Love is not just an attribute of God; it is the essence of God. Love is the foundational, core Reality of the universe. If we are to become

---

1. Borg, *The Heart of Christianity*, 72.
2. Ibid., 72.

the persons we were created to be, then we must live connected to and grounded in the Divine Love that is God. When we open our hearts to love, we open our hearts to God and to an authentic human life.

In the movie, *Tuesdays with Morrie,* based on the book by the same name, sports writer, Mitch Albom, makes a number of visits to his former college professor and friend, Morrie Schwartz, who is dying of ALS. In these visits Mitch learns some important lessons about what really matters in life. In one encounter Morrie says, "When we're infants we need people to survive; when we're dying we need people to survive; but here's the secret—in between, we need each other even more." Mitch nods and replies with a phrase that he has heard Morrie say many times, "We must love each other or die."

Morrie retorts, "Yeah, but do you believe that? Does it apply to you?" Mitch, somewhat defensively, acknowledges that he doesn't know what he believes. Morrie probes, "You hate that word, don't you—spiritual? You think it's just touchy-feely stuff, huh?" Mitch says, "I just don't understand it." Morrie repeats, "We must love one another or die. It's a very simple lesson, Mitch."[3]

In John's Gospel, Jesus says to his disciples, "This is my commandment, that you love one another as I have loved you" (John 15:12). In the broader context of that passage Jesus/John offers instruction in discipleship by drawing an analogy to a grape vine and its branches.[4] Fruitful branches draw their vitality and nourishment from the life that flows through the vine. Branches severed from the vine wither and die. Disciples who live fruitful, healthy, productive lives "abide" (remain, dwell, make their home) in Christ's love, the love he received from God. Jesus says, "Abide in me as I abide in you. Just as the branch cannot bear fruit by itself unless it abides in the vine, neither can you unless you abide in me . . . As the Father loved me, so I have loved you; abide in my love" (John 15:4, 9). Disciples of Jesus experience an abundant, meaningful, personal and communal life through their connection to God's love in Christ.

---

3. *Tuedsays with Morrie,* Touchstone, 1999.

4. Practically all Johannine scholars acknowledge that the discourses attributed to Jesus in John's Gospel reflect the theological and spiritual interpretations of the Johannine community. Some scholars would assign the discourses in their entirety to the Johannine writer/community. My position is that the discourses attributed to Jesus by John are expositions and elaborations by the writer or community of authentic short sayings of Jesus.

New Testament scholar and former preaching professor, Dr. Fred Craddock tells about the time, some years ago, when he was preaching at a church in Tennessee. There was a girl about seven years old who came for Sunday School and sometimes her parents let her stay for worship. Her parents didn't attend. They had moved from New Jersey to work at the new chemical plant. They were both very ambitious, upwardly mobile, and never felt a need for church.

On Saturday nights they hosted parties, not for entertainment, but as the upwardly mobile thing to do. They invited the right people—the ones just above them on the corporate ladder, and finally on up to the boss. But every Sunday their beautiful daughter was in church.

One Sunday morning Dr. Craddock looked out and thought, "Well, she's with her friends," but it was her mother and father. After the sermon, at the close of the service when an invitation to discipleship was extended, Mr. and Mrs. Mom and Dad walked to the front. They confessed faith in and commitment to Christ. Afterward Dr. Craddock asked, "What prompted this commitment?"

They said, "Well, we had a party again last night, and it got a little loud, and it got a little rough, and there was too much drinking. Our daughter awoke and came downstairs to about the third step. She saw that we were eating and drinking, and she said, 'Oh, can I say the blessing? God is great, God is good, let us thank him for our food. Good night, everybody.' Then she went back upstairs. Someone said, 'Oh, my land, its time to go.' Someone else said, 'We've stayed too long.' Within two minutes the room was empty."

Mr. and Mrs. Mom and Dad began cleaning up, picking up crumpled napkins, spilled peanuts, half sandwiches, and taking empty glasses on trays to the kitchen. Each with a tray, Mom and Dad met at the sink. They looked at each other, and he expressed what both were thinking, "Where do we think we're going?"[5]

They came to the startling realization that they were investing their lives in the wrong kind of connections. What kind of connections do we have? Are they the kind of connections that will get us someplace in the world—the kind that will advance our upward mobility? The kind of connections we most need are the kind that will enable us to experience the Divine Reality of Love that became incarnate in Jesus, who as the living Christ invites us now to learn from him how to know and experience the transforming power of love.

5. Craddock, *Craddock Stories*, 23–24.

LIVING OUT OF THE CENTER

Franciscan priest and spiritual writer, Richard Rohr says, "We are a circumference people, with little access to the center. We live on the boundaries of our own lives 'in the widening gyre,' confusing edges with essence, too quickly claiming the superficial as substance."[6] Rohr contends that the circumferences, or edges of our lives, are not necessarily bad or evil, but they are passing, fleeting, and illusory—they lack substance. To live for money, pleasure, success, control, or honor and fame, does not enable us to reach our potential as human beings. When these things dominate our minds and pervade our hearts, we are not living out of our center, out of the true self.

We are easily swayed and deceived when we live at the circumference level of life. The negative forces of consumerism, militarism, racism, sexism, narcissism, and rampant individualism can overwhelm us like a tidal wave, dumping us out on a shore of meaninglessness and despair. We need a center out of which to live; a core with substance that will give true meaning to our lives, enabling us to live an authentic human existence.

The phrase "eternal life" (or simply "life") that is found numerous times in John's Gospel refers primarily, I believe, to authentic human life. It is unfortunate that many Christians have put the emphasis on the duration of life, making it exclusively a reference to the afterlife in heaven. Certainly the phrase implies that the spiritual life mediated through Christ is endless in duration, but that aspect is not its most important or primary meaning. In John 17, Jesus says, "And this is eternal life, that they may know you, the only true God, and Jesus Christ whom you have sent" (John 17:3). In John 10, Jesus declares, "I came that they may have life, and have it abundantly" (John 10:10). The primary meaning of "life" or "eternal life" in John's Gospel relates to a particular kind or quality of life. It is life oriented around and centered upon God's new world. (I will develop this vision of the kingdom of God in chapter 2). It is life lived in a healthy, holistic, transformative relationship with God and with others for the good of humankind and the creation. It is life lived out of the center.

John's Gospel also emphasizes that eternal life—life lived out of the center, authentic human existence, life that revolves around God's kingdom—is appropriated and experienced by faith. In perhaps the most

---

6. Rohr, *Everything Belongs*, 13.

well known verse in all the Bible, John says, "For God so loved the world that he gave his only Son, so that everyone who believes in him may not perish but may have eternal life" (John 3:16). So how does this work?

First and foremost, disciples of Jesus claim by faith their true identity. They trust God to name them. They discover their identity and security, not out on the edges of their lives, but in God who lives within them.

Until we find our center in God and in God's will for our lives, we will not even know what boundaries are worth defending. Richard Rohr points out that one of the most obvious indicators of non-centered people is that they are, quite frankly, difficult to live with. All their ego boundaries have to be defended—"their reputation, their needs, their nation, their security, their religion, even their ball team."[7] When people find that they are frequently hurt or offended, that's a good sign that they are living out on the circumference, and not out of the center.

We are living on the circumference if we allow other people to name and define who we are. In a "Peanuts" comic strip, Lucy is sitting in a little booth where a "Doctor Is In" sign is prominently displayed. Of course, Charlie Brown visits Lucy. She says to him, "You know what your problem is, Charlie Brown? The problem with you is that you're you." Crushed, Charlie Brown asks, "Well, what in the world can I do about that?" Lucy responds in the final frame, "I don't pretend to be able to give advice. I merely point out the problem."

If we have been ignored or made to feel like an invisible presence or rejected as a nobody, we might come to internalize Lucy's diagnosis: "the problem is that you are you." If we hear that enough or if, for whatever reason, we have procured a fragile self-image, we might start believing it. If we believe that lie, there is a good chance we will live on the circumference, pursuing ego-needs in order to feel good about ourselves and to prove that it's not true. Or maybe we become convinced that it is true and that we can do nothing about it, so we give up in defeat or succumb to shame and self-hate. Then we drift along, living from one fix, one high, one affair, one peak experience to the next in order to numb the pain.

According to a Greek legend, Helen of Troy was kidnapped and whisked across the seas to a distant city. Though she managed to escape from her captors, she suffered from amnesia and became a prostitute in the streets. Back in her homeland, her friends kept searching for her. One admiring adventurer who never lost faith set out on a journey to find her

---

7. Ibid., 25.

and bring her back. One day as he was wandering through the streets of a strange city, he came across a prostitute who looked strangely familiar. When asked about her identity, she responded with a meaningless name. He asked, "Can I see your hands?" He knew the lines of Helen's hands. When he studied her hands he exclaimed, "You are Helen! You are Helen of Troy!" "Helen?" she replied. When she spoke her name the fog began to clear and a sense of recognition registered on her face. She embraced her old friend and wept, having discovered her true self. She discarded her old clothes and her old life, and embarked upon a new adventure of becoming the queen she was called to be.

When William Sloan Coffin was chaplain at Yale, it was natural for seniors bound for graduate school to come to him for letters of recommendation to such preeminent schools as Harvard Law School or Columbia Medical School. In his recommendation he would often have to inform the school that, most likely, the candidate would land somewhere in the bottom quarter of his or her class. However, many times he had the privilege of telling them that the candidate would seek the common good over personal gain, would strive to be valuable rather than successful, and would strive to make a difference rather than accumulate a lot of money. Coffin would then argue that the student embodying these virtues was eminently qualified for admission into their school.

Invariably, when the letter was shown to the student, the student's feelings would be hurt. The student would say, "How do you know I'm going to be in the bottom of the class?" Coffin would respond, "Well, all the evidence is in, isn't it?" The student would retort, "Yes, but you didn't have to tell them." Coffin observed,

> You see what was going on? Never mind that I enumerated some sterling extracurricular qualities. Never mind that in order to be accepted into Harvard Law or Columbia Medical you had to be in the ninety-seventh percentile and to graduate in the ninety-eighth. Just because I didn't say they would be in the ninety-ninth percentile, they felt they had somehow failed. Such is the power of higher education to tell you who you are![8]

Is our identity tied to our accomplishments and honors, our education, our performance vocationally, academically, or athletically, our money or status in the community? To whom do we look for approval and acceptance? Who tells us who we are?

8. Coffin, *Letters to a Young Doubter*, 8–9.

If we are to live out of the center, if we are to live an authentic human existence and discover our true selves, then we must claim by faith who we are. We must claim our identity as the beloved daughters and sons of God.

We are loved and called by God to be friends of God and of Christ. Jesus says to his disciples in John 15, "I have called you friends, for everything that I learned from my Father I have made known to you" (John 15:15, TNIV). Jesus shared with his disciples what he knew about God; he considered them to be his friends, his brothers and sisters in the family of God and partners in God's redemptive mission.

In the same passage Jesus says, "You do not belong to the world, I have chosen you out of the world" (John 15:19, TNIV). Jesus does not divide people into "us" and "them," but Jesus does make a clear distinction between the identity thrust upon us by the principalities and powers of the world and our true identity as God's children and as Christ's friends.

This is not something we have to earn or achieve; it is a gift. It is our birthright. We are born of God. There are no preconditions—no believing the right things or joining the right church. We are accepted, loved, and forgiven. Christians experience this grace through Christ.

John, in his prologue says, "to all who received Christ (the Word made flesh, full of grace and truth), to all who trusted in the word and character of Christ, to these God gave the right, power, and authority to become children of God" (John 1:12–13, my paraphrase). Those who nurture a dynamic trust in Jesus Christ and commitment to his way in the world discover the power to become who they are.

Christians discover an infinite reservoir of grace in Christ. Christ embodies, reveals, and mediates God's grace to his followers. In a relationship with Christ, disciples experience God's acceptance, forgiveness, and abundant provision for life. John says, "Out of his fullness we have all received grace in place of grace already given" (John 1:16, TNIV). When one provision of grace is received, there is another to take its place—there is no end to the supply of God's love and grace for human need.

We can live an authentic and flourishing human existence by claiming through faith our true identity as children of God. This involves a decision to love.

Love functions as the foundation for faith and is also the means by which our faith is expressed. In his letter to the Galatians, Paul contends that the only thing that really counts is faith expressing itself through love (Gal 5:6). Faith links our present day experience, whether ecstatic or tragic, wonderful or terrible, to the Divine Goodness at the heart of life itself. Faith enables us to weave the fragments of our experience into a greater whole; to connect our little stories to a greater story where Love will ultimately triumph (I expound upon this theme in chapter 3).

Unlike the kid with his face pressed up against the bakery window with no money and no resources to access any of the goodies he sees and craves inside, by faith we have access to the Divine Love that creates, sustains, and persuasively (not coercively) directs all creation in an ever new, fresh, unfolding adventure of becoming.[9] God's Spirit is within each of us and the fruit of the Spirit is, first and foremost, love (Gal 5:22).

Love is a choice. Every day we must choose forgiveness over resentment, grace over guilt, mercy over condemnation, kindness over apathy, faith over fear, and hope over despair. We either push God away by choosing not to love, or we draw near to God by choosing to love. When we choose to love, we align ourselves with God's renewing, healing purpose and God's redemptive power is unleashed within us. When we choose not to love, when the ego leads us in a different direction, we close ourselves off to God's redeeming power in our lives.

A number of years ago when the miracle of electricity had only recently become available, a very affluent, but frugal, elderly woman decided to have electricity brought into her house. A month after she had tapped into this great source of power a workman from the electric company came to her house to read the meter. Thinking there must be a problem, he inquired about her electricity usage. She explained that in the evenings she turned on her electric lights only long enough to light her candles, and then quickly turned them back off. The power was available, but she rarely tapped into it. We have been wired by our Creator to love and through Christ we connect to the ultimate source of Love. But we must choose to utilize this power and to live out of the center. We must choose to deny our self-centered ego desires and actively engage in acts and deeds of love.

Will we fail? Of course. The journey into the heart and essence of life will be more arduous for some than others. It will be especially challenging for those who never received much love or affirmation from family and peers. All of us to some degree are enslaved to our ego addictions and attachments, and to self-centered, ingrained patterns of liv-

9. An excellent spiritual resource on this theme is Bruce Epperly, *Holy Adventure*.

ing and negative habits of reacting. We may have deep-seated guilt and resentment issues to resolve. The ability to break free from entrenched behaviors, addictions, and attitudes will not come easy. And when we find ourselves making the same mistakes over and over, failing to love well, we can easily get flustered and frustrated.

A little girl learned in Sunday School the Bible verse that says, "So let your light shine before others that they may see your good works and glorify your Father in heaven." When she got home she asked her mother what it meant. Her mother told her that it meant that when she lets Jesus live in her heart, the light of his love and goodness shines upon all those around her.

The very next week in Sunday School the same little girl got caught up in an argument with another child in the class. She became so out-of-sorts that the teacher had to go get her mother. Her mother said, "Sweetie, don't you remember about letting your light shine before others." The little girl blurted out, "I know mommy, I just blowed myself out!" I'm sure there are times when we have all felt that way after we have failed to reflect the love of God in our words or actions. But when we fail it does no good to linger there, loathing and despising ourselves.

Frank Laubach was a sociologist, educator, and missionary to the Philippines in the early twentieth century. When he was in his forties his life and career fell apart. He lost the vocational opportunity he most desired. His plans for the Maranao people were utterly rejected. He and his wife lost three children to malaria. His wife packed up and took their remaining child a thousand miles away, leaving him desperately lonely. At the brink of despair, he took his dog Tip and went to the top of Signal Hill overlooking Lake Lanao. He wrote in his journal,

> Tip has his nose up under my arm and was trying to lick the tears off my cheeks. My lips began to move and it seemed to me that God was speaking. My child . . . you have failed because you do not really love these Maranaos. You feel superior to them because you are white. If you forget you are an American and think only of how I love them, they will respond. I answered back to the sunset, "God, I don't know whether you spoke to me through my lips, but if you did, it was the truth. My plans have all gone to pieces. Drive me out of myself and come and take possession of me and think thy thoughts in my mind."[10]

---

10. Referenced in Ortburg, *If You Want to Walk on Water*, 164.

Frank Laubach went on to become a world statesman. He founded the World Literacy Crusade, and without any political appointment, became influential on United States foreign policy in the post-World War II years. Through his constant interaction with God he adopted the philosophy of instantaneous new beginnings. If God forgives us instantly and completely, then who are we to sulk in despair over our failures? If God finds no pleasure in condemning, then we have no right to find some sort of sadistic pleasure in self-contempt. To allow the sins of yesterday, or even an hour ago, to rob our joy in life and send us on a downward spiral of self-condemnation is to refuse to believe and claim God's unconditional love and forgiveness. We are called to live in this present moment, to meet God in the now, and to invite God to engender in us a deep gratitude for God's overflowing grace. Such gratitude enables us to be conduits of this grace as we live attuned to the needs all around us and to the movement of God's Spirit in and through us.

Author and Buddhist teacher, Sharon Salzberg was teaching a meditation class at a women's prison in California some years ago. One of the inmates observed, "When you're in prison, it's especially important to try to live in the present moment. It's easy to get lost in the past, which you can't change anyway, or to get lost hoping for the future, which is not yet here. If you do that, it's like you're not really alive." Then she paused and declared, her eyes glimmering, "I choose life."[11]

Salzberg once asked a psychiatrist friend what he considered the single most compelling force for healing in the psychotherapeutic relationship. "Love," was his response. She agreed with him, but then wondered if there wasn't something else even more fundamental, like showing up for one's appointment. We affirm life by believing that we are capable of learning how to love, and by "showing up" each day ready to grow in our capacity to love.

What will we choose? Will we yield to the powers that be and allow their voices to name and shape us, or will we claim by faith our identity as the daughters and sons of God? Will we choose to live on the edges by defending our selfish ambitions and by manipulating people and plans for our own pleasure and glory, or will we choose to live out of the center by loving one another in thought, word, and deed? The seed for a life rich and abundant in love is within us. With a little bit of faith that seed can take root and flourish.

11. Salzberg, *Faith*, 15.

A NEW KIND OF ORTHODOXY

When we choose to love, our spiritual eyes are opened and we are given fresh insights into the holistic and healing nature of Divine Realty. The story of the healing of the blind man in chapter 9 of John's Gospel illustrates this beautifully.

The story begins with Jesus "seeing" a man born blind. The disciples accompanying Jesus do not really "see" him; in their view he is merely the subject for a theological discussion. They ask Jesus, "Rabbi, who sinned, this man or his parents?" (9:2). Their question is based on a popular belief that attributed sickness and unfortunate circumstances to the hand of God. The disciples think they can "see," but they are actually blind to the truth.

We are all children of our culture. We tend to believe things, not because we have carefully thought about them, not because we have studied, reflected, and critically assessed them, but because we have grown up with them, or were taught them in our churches or by our parents, or maybe they were simply the prevailing beliefs among our friends and peers. We internalize beliefs and form a worldview quite naturally through a process of socialization within our culture.

My early Christian training involved indoctrination into a particular belief system. Some of the teachings were good and helpful, while other aspects were not conducive to a healthy spirituality. At an early age, some unhealthy biases, detrimental to the vision of God's new world, became ingrained in my thinking through an informational based process of Christian education.

Churches could nurture healthier, more compassionate Christians if they taught their members and participants less about *what* to believe and invested more time in teaching them *how* to believe. I like the way Christian theologian and philosopher, Peter Rollins redefines an orthodox Christian. He has argued that a truly orthodox Christian is not one who believes all the right things, but one who believes in the right way—that is, believing in a loving, sacrificial, and Christ-like manner.[12] The call and challenge of discipleship to Jesus is not one of guarding or capsulating the truth by reducing it to theological propositions, but rather, one of incarnating the truth by exuding Christ's love and compassion.

---

12. Rollins, *How (Not) to Speak of God*, 2–3.

Jesus heals the blind man, and because it is the Sabbath, some of the Pharisees who see themselves as the guardians of the Torah become angry with Jesus for violating Sabbath law. As the story unfolds, the Pharisees first question the man who was healed, then they call in his parents and question them, and finally, they call back the man who was healed for a second round of interrogations.

In the second round of questioning, the man who was healed responds courageously to their verbal assaults. The Pharisees accuse Jesus of being a sinner and when the healed man objects, they say to him, "You were born entirely in sins, and are you trying to teach us?" (9:34). Then they excommunicate him from the synagogue community.

The gradual awakening of the healed man's spiritual sight contrasts sharply with the increased animosity and hardening unbelief of the religious leaders' spiritual blindness. Preaching professor and biblical scholar, Thomas Long calls this "a collision of moral worlds" and illustrates by referring to the trial of the Berrigan brothers.

In May of 1968 two Roman Catholic priests, Daniel and Philip Berrigan, and seven of their Christian friends—two missionaries, a midwife, a nurse, a worker in race relations, and two others—walked into the draft board office in Catonsville, Maryland at the height of the Vietnam War. As an act of nonviolent protest and witness for peace, they took some draft files out of a filing cabinet, carried them out into the street, and burned them. They were, of course, arrested and charged with a federal crime.

In October of that year they were placed on trial in federal court in Baltimore. "Why did you do this?" said the prosecutor to Daniel Berrigan. "I did it," he said, "because I began to see the cost of being a Christian. When I saw the napalm kill children, my senses were invaded; and I saw the power of death in the modern world." At this point the judge interrupted, "Father Berrigan. This testimony is irrelevant. The war is not on trial, you are." "Your Honor," replied Daniel Berrigan, "I can only tell you what I see, and what I see is that right now we are standing before the living God." One of the attorneys said, "Mr. Berrigan, are you saying your religious convictions had something to do with this?" Berrigan responded, "Yes, yes, of course my religious convictions had something to do with this. If it were not for my religious convictions, this would be eviscerated of meaning; and I should be committed for insanity."

Another defendant, Mary Marlin, a nurse, stood up and said, "I did this because I have begun to see things as they are. This is what a Christian does when you see things." She turned to the judge and said, "Your Honor, you stand well for the law, but what about God's law of peace?" The judge puzzled over this a minute and then said, "Uh, I see your point," then he hesitated and said, "but you are not my spiritual advisor."[13]

As we are drawn to the light, as our minds and hearts become illuminated by the light of the grace and truth of Christ, a collision of moral worlds is inevitable. We can no longer be content with the world as it is, not when we are given a vision of what the world can be. The more we are drawn into the light of Christ, the less we can rest easy or feel comfortable in the world as it is. The light of humility, grace, and truth incarnate in Christ and his followers exposes the injustice, prejudice, and greed of the domination system. John's Gospel, in its rich symbolism, explains the collision this way,

> And this is the judgment, that the light has come into the world, and people loved darkness rather than light because their deeds were evil. For all who do evil hate the light and do not come to the light, so that their deeds may not be exposed. But those who do what is true come to the light, so that it may be clearly seen that their deeds have been done in God. John 3:19–21

Many modern Christian testimonies narrate how Jesus has rescued them from their guilt and given them new meaning and purpose in life. However true that may be, too often such testimonies leave the impression that when we come to know Christ our troubles will end. This Americanized version of Christianity as a religion of comfort is fed and fueled by the goals and priorities of our consumerist culture. We have a propensity for Christianizing our desires to acquire, consume, and control. We dress them up in religious garb and use them to justify our greed and selfish ambition. We allow the market values of our culture to bleed over into our spiritual life, blinding us to what is true and what has inherent value.

When our eyes are opened and we are able to see these egocentric interests for what they are, a collision of moral worlds occurs. No longer can we acquiesce to our culture and continue to live unmoved when we see injustice, or when we see how religion is used to advance the agenda of the powerful, or when we see how the radical Jesus is domesticated

---

13. Long, "Once I Was Blind," 55–56.

and rendered harmless by much of Christendom. Once we can see, life will never be the same again.

This collision occurs at all levels of reality, particularly in our own innermost nature. Our capacity to see both truth and illusion, good and evil in the world usually expands in proportion to our capacity to see such things in our own lives. The evil and illusions of our world cut through every human heart.

The religious leaders in John 9 see sin everywhere but in themselves. In the final line of the story, Jesus says to the Pharisees, "If you were blind, you would not have sin. But now that you say, 'We see,' your sin remains" (9:41).

The assumption that we already know blocks spiritual teaching and keeps us in the dark. Healthy religion never claims certainty. It confesses to being blind. A humble approach is required to nurture honest, sincere seekers of God, who even when they experience God's love know that God is always beyond them, greater than what they can imagine, comprehend, or feel.

Unhealthy religion spins a false confidence that results in spiritual arrogance. It creates people who think they have God in their pockets. They dismiss their critics with glib, simplistic answers and become spiritual gatekeepers claiming to know who's "in" and "out," who's saved and unsaved, who's blessed and cursed. Immense harm is done by people who presume to see, but are really blind.

The more we abide in God's love and live out of the center, the greater our capacity to see what's real and to humbly live compassionate, communal lives of meaning and significance.

A LIVING FAITH

When we live out of our connection to the Divine Goodness that pervades the universe, we are free to question our beliefs and allow them to evolve as we grow in our experience and understanding of God's magnanimous love.

Maggie Dawn, writing in *The Christian Century*, tells about reading Roald Dahl's, *The BFG* ("The Big Friendly Giant"), to her son. Giants are suppose to be "terrible, blood-thirsty creatures" so when little Sophie is kidnapped by a giant in the middle of the night and carried far away to a land where giants live, naturally she is terrified. "He is getting ready to eat me, she tells herself. He will probably eat me raw, just as I am. Or perhaps he will boil me first."

As the story unfolds, Sophie discovers that her giant is actually quite nice. She has nothing to fear from this giant. Dawn observes, "What she saw and what she thought she saw were not the same thing at all."[14] Dawn writes,

> Encountering God in depth inevitably means that we have to unlearn a lot of ideas that are deeply ingrained in us, but which may be at odds with the truth. We draw our idea of God from a mixture of sources, often unconsciously; from childhood experiences, from media, from things we have heard or misheard in church, read or misread in the scriptures. This collection of ideas is the baggage we bring with us to faith, so that God becomes, in our experience, a mixture of truth and misconception. The God we expect to meet may not be the God we actually encounter.[15]

In the movie, *The Truman Show*, Truman Burbank (played by Jim Carrey) lives in an artificially contrived world. The entire town is dedicated to a continually running TV show. Everyone except Truman is an actor. For Truman it's all real, until something inside him begins to tell him that there must be something more.

Truman encounters many obstacles in his attempt to break out of his box: traffic jams, the inability to book flights, the bus breaks down when he buys a bus ticket out of town, etc. In the final scene he overcomes his fear of water and sails against a hurricane force wind. When he reaches the edge of his world, he exits via a door in the wall (painted to look like the sky) to the thrill of the television audience. Truman leaves behind the artificial world that entrapped him and discovers the reality of a whole new world.[16]

I have no doubt that many persons of faith have become trapped in worlds imposed upon them by their religious upbringing—religious traditions, institutions, and authorities that have been instrumental in shaping their faith. Like Truman, they believe that their thoughts and beliefs are the product of their own will and initiative, but actually their world is defined by patterns and beliefs that have been profoundly socialized and ingrained in them. Most of us are either born into a faith tradition

---

14. Dawn, "Faith Matters: Second Thoughts," 37.
15. Ibid., 37.
16. *The Truman Show*, Paramount Pictures, 1998.

or converted into one, and that's all we know until we start to think for ourselves—questioning, reasoning, and comparing truth claims.

In John's Gospel, when Nathanael is told by Philip that he has found the Messiah, Jesus of Nazareth, the son of Joseph, his initial response is, "Can anything good come out of Nazareth?" (John 1:46). According to Johannine scholar R. E. Brown, the saying by Nathanael may echo a local proverb that expressed some animosity and disdain between Nathanael's town of Cana and nearby Nazareth.[17] Nathanael's reaction most likely reflects a prejudicial, contemptuous belief that he had been taught as a child and was reinforced in his community.

As the narrative unfolds, Jesus proceeds to shatter that belief. I wonder how many of us find ourselves stuck in our spiritual lives because we cling to unhealthy beliefs that have come to define and confine our religious worlds. Nathanael had to let go of this negative belief before he could see from a more positive and honest perspective.

When I share my own faith journey I like to say that this is what I believe right now, at this stage in my pilgrimage, but I could be wrong. Unless I am willing to admit that I could be wrong, I have no real hope of seeing with new eyes or experiencing God in new ways. Unless I can humbly admit my limitations as a human being seeking truth, I will never discover and actualize truth. This is why some people remain blind to spiritual truth; they require certainty. They cannot bear to admit that they could be wrong, even though we all see through a glass dimly.

Those who cling to rigid, narrow systems of belief often do so out of fear and insecurity. A natural response to fear is to cling to something. For a baby this natural instinct can be a healthy reflex, but for persons of faith it can stunt our growth and keep us spiritual infants. The more we cling to a rigid set of beliefs the less faith and courage we need to trust the Divine Love who strengthens and sustains us. Religious adherents who seem compulsive in their efforts to convince and convert others to their belief system are most likely to be persons, to use a phrase of Jesus, "of little faith."

When we allow fixed beliefs to determine reality for us, it's like gazing at the sky through a straw (a Buddhist analogy). Looking through a straw we have only a small, limited field of sight. Yet we cling to our limited vision as if it defines and explains all reality. We even become

---

17. Brown, *The Gospel According to John, I–XII*, 83.

defensive, claiming that our straws offer a more reliable and accurate vision than the straws used by other people of faith.[18]

Sharon Salzberg says that when she first began teaching meditation with Joseph Goldstein at Naropa University in Boulder, Colorado, she had very little self-confidence. In order to hide her fear, she answered questions with great conviction, quoting from text and tradition, but not really speaking out of her own experience. She had a difficult time dealing with conflicting traditions.

She had practiced her faith in the context of Theravada Buddhism, which is prevalent in Burma, Thailand, and other countries of Southeast Asia. Naropa Univerity, founded by the Tibetan Trungpa Rinpoche, is aligned with Mahayana Buddhism. The Theravadan view of the afterlife conflicts with the Tibetan view. Theravadans believe that when one dies, the person is reborn the very next moment. The Tibetans, however, believe that one goes though the phases of a *bardo*, an intermediate stage, before rebirth.

One day a student in the Tibetan tradition challenged her belief in the afterlife. The two of them were all alone in a sparsely furnished room. As the two of them arduously defended their positions her opponent became angrier and angrier. Eventually, he lost his temper, accusing her of being a liar. "In a way," says Salzberg, "he was right. I had no real knowledge of what happens after death, no matter what any tradition says, and I was too afraid to simply say, 'I don't know.'" Salzberg remarks, "The mind's determination to see things a certain way transforms fear into hostility. It is likely that the man at Naropa University and I were fundamentally just people afraid to die.[19]

A belief is the result of our attempt to grasp or explain something at a given point in time. Every belief comes wrapped in the cultural package of a particular time and place, which is why our beliefs need to be constantly revisited and reassessed. If our faith, however, is rooted and grounded in the Divine Goodness that sustains and supports all life, then we are free to question our beliefs without any fear or anxiety of offending God. Do our beliefs help us to recognize pride, prejudice, and greed,

---

18. There are appropriate times and places to debate faith perspectives and the redemptive visions they cast. Certainly not all belief systems have equal credibility. But such dialogue and debate must be entered into with humility and a readiness to learn, not defensively or arrogantly, insisting on the absoluteness of one's faith claims. I will say more about this in chapter 3.

19. Salzberg, *Faith*, 64–66.

not just in others, but especially in ourselves? Do our beliefs advance a humility and openness of heart and soul that nurtures our own personal transformation into more loving, compassionate persons? Do our beliefs ignite participation in issues and actions of restorative justice, peacemaking, and inclusive mercy that will contribute to the health, healing, and wholeness of communities and societies on earth?

A living faith is a transformative response to the faithfulness of God's love. It involves a deepening trust in the goodness, faithfulness, and love of God, rather than simple adherence to a collection of religious beliefs. Healthy beliefs, though, will inspire, sustain, and advance a vibrant faith that drives out fear and defensiveness. Brother David Steindl-Rast expressed it this way,

> The faith of the heart, our primordial faith, is something we have all experienced in our peak moments of aliveness. How did we experience it? As simple trust, as confidence: trust in life; confidence that we won't be let down. At those moments, when we live from our heart, we are in touch with the heart of things. Spontaneously we realize: "There is faithfulness at the heart of all things," as Oscar Cullmann put it so well. Spoken or unspoken, this conviction of faith is the root from which our beliefs spring. It is the touchstone also to test beliefs. If they are genuine, they will express that core conviction and so serve as helpful reminders. Beliefs can never replace the experience of live faith, but they can help us keep it alive.[20]

A living faith involves a courageous trust in God's basic goodness and providential care. Jesus described faith this way,

> Therefore I tell you, do not worry about your life, what you will eat or what you will drink, or about your body, what you will wear. Is not life more than food, and the body more than clothing? Look at the birds of the air; they neither sow nor reap nor gather into barns, and yet your heavenly Father feeds then. Are you not of more value than they? And can any of you by worrying add a single hour to your span of life? And why do you worry about clothing? Consider the lilies of the field, how they grow; they neither toil nor spin, yet I tell you, even Solomon in all his glory was not clothed like one of these. But if God so clothes the grass of the field, which is alive today and tomorrow is thrown

---

20. Steindl-Rast, *Gratefulness, the Heart of Prayer*, 102.

> into the oven, will he not much more clothe you—you of little faith? (Matt 6:25–30)

The acid test for any theology (worldview and set of beliefs) is its portrayal of the character and nature of Divine Reality. If the God imagined and described in our belief system is not the kind of God who commends our devotion and commitment, then we need to reexamine and refine our belief system. Healthy beliefs are flexible and fluid enough to change shape and form, and still nurture and strengthen a courageous faith.

A living faith connects us with the core of Divine Reality that in the best of the Christian tradition affirms, "God is love. Whoever lives in love lives in God, and God in them . . . There is no fear in love. But perfect love drives out fear . . ." (1 John 4:16, 18). Such faith opens our minds and widens our hearts; it expands our imagination and enlarges our hospitality. A living faith inspires contagious joy, abounding gratitude, and deep compassion.

SURVIVING THE STORMS

A multifaceted theological story relating to faith is found in Matthew 14:22–33. Jesus sent the disciples across the Sea of Galilee while he dismissed the crowds and ascended "the mountain by himself to pray" (14:23). The disciples encountered difficulty navigating across because their boat was "battered by waves" and the "wind was against them" (14:24). In the early morning, Jesus came to them walking on the water. When the disciples first glimpsed Jesus coming towards them "they were terrified," thinking he was a ghost. Jesus said, "Take heart, it is I; do not be afraid." Unique to Matthew's version of the story is the interchange between Jesus and Peter,

> Peter answered him, "Lord, if it is you, command me to come to you on the water." He said, "Come." So Peter got out of the boat, started walking on the water, and came toward Jesus. But when he noticed the strong wind, he became frightened, and beginning to sink, he cried out, "Lord, save me!" Jesus immediately reached out his hand and caught him, saying to him, "You of little faith, why did you doubt?" When they got into the boat, the wind ceased. And those in the boat worshiped him, saying, "Truly you are the Son of God." Matt 14:28–33

Theologian and Christian minister, John Killinger told about turning on the television one morning while exercising. A merchant of self-confidence was trying to sell people a set of tapes on how to be successful in business. He began by saying that the most incontrovertible thing about anyone is a person's behavior—how a person conducts himself or herself. Then he said that feelings lie behind and determine behavior; if a person feels a certain way, that person is likely to act a certain way. Then he said that behind feelings are attitudes; attitudes influence feelings. If a person has a positive attitude, then most likely that person will feel good about herself or himself, and generally feel good about his or her relationship with others. Next, he said that behind a person's attitude is what a person believes. Belief determines attitudes, which determine feelings, which determine behavior. Killinger thought he would stop there, but he didn't. He went on to suggest that belief is not the final determinant; that behind what a person believes is the programming that person has received. He argued that we believe what we are programmed to believe.

Certainly this chain of response is a rather simplistic explanation that cannot possibly account for or explain all actions, feelings, attitudes, and beliefs. But there is some truth in it. What we believe does indeed impact what we think, feel, and do. Small children, for example, believe certain things because they have been programmed to believe them. Of course, as they learn to think for themselves, they become open to new programming from teachers, peers, professors, religious instructors, the media, as well as any number of social and cultural influences. As a general rule, a person is more likely to believe certain things when several sources of influence reinforce the same or similar beliefs. This is true of both healthy and unhealthy beliefs. For example, racist and sexist beliefs are most likely sustained in a context where one's parents and peers maintain and practice such beliefs, and one's culture reinforces them.[21]

There are powerful forces at work in our world set against the development of a healthy religious faith. Doubt, however, need not be one of them. If doubt causes us to question and discard negative, unhealthy, destructive beliefs, then doubt is a beneficial and life-enhancing experience. In my own faith journey, had I not felt comfortable with doubt, I probably would no longer be in the pastoral ministry. My doubt ignited

---

21. Patriarchal beliefs, for example, are often reflected in the biblical traditions because they were so dominant in the culture of biblical times. Yet, within the biblical texts there are significant challenges to patriarchy as some biblical writers and communities caught a more egalitarian vision. Some individuals and communities are able to rise above and offer a prophetic witness against unhealthy, biased beliefs that pervade a culture.

a passion to study, reflect, question, and think more deeply and critically about my faith. My doubt did not cause me to abandon my faith in God, though it did press me to relinquish prior understandings of God that I no longer found acceptable. It prompted me to explore my faith and led me to embrace a more inclusive, gracious, and intellectually credible faith. Doubt was God's means of grace in my life to nurture a more substantive understanding of God and a deeper discipleship to Christ.

At the end of Matthew's Gospel, the risen Christ meets the eleven on a mountain in Galilee. Matthew says, "When they saw him, they worshiped him; but some doubted" (Matt 28:17). They were not rejected or even criticized for their doubt, and all of them (doubters included) were given a new mission with the promise of the presence of the risen Christ (28:18–20). Doubt is destructive to faith only when it propels us to jettison healthy beliefs and adopt a cynical attitude toward life. Reconstruction requires some deconstruction.

What caused Peter to sink and what prompted Jesus' question, "Why did you doubt?" A common homiletical interpretation is that Peter started to sink because he took his eyes off Jesus. That's not, however, what the text says. The text reads, "But when he noticed the strong wind, he became frightened, and beginning to sink, he cried out, 'Lord, save me!'" (Matt 14:30). The text doesn't say that he took his eyes off Jesus; it says that when he saw the wind, fear gripped him. Fear is not the direct opposite of faith—one can be afraid and still have faith—but fear can overwhelm, diminish, and stifle faith.

The story is told that when Teddy Roosevelt was a young boy he was afraid to go into church alone. He was terrified of something he called the "zeal." He imagined it crouched in the dark corners of the church building ready to pounce on and devour him. When his mother asked what he thought this "zeal" was he wasn't sure, but he pictured it as a large animal like an alligator or dragon. He heard the minister speak about it from the Bible. Using a concordance, his mother looked up the passages that contained this word and read them to him. When she read the text from John 2:17, he told her to stop. The text reads in the King James Version, "And his disciples remembered that it was written, 'The zeal of thine house hath eaten me up.'" This sort of fear is faith suffocating.

The movie, *Hoosiers*, is a Cinderella story of a small town basketball team from Hickory Indiana that overcomes adversity to win the state championship. Norman Dale (played by Gene Hackman), a former college coach with a troubled past, is the coach that leads them to victory. When the team arrives at Butler Field House in Indianapolis to play for the State Championship their jaws drop. They are overwhelmed at the huge arena with its freestanding hoops and suspended backboards. They seem suddenly paralyzed by fear.

I know that feeling. My little high school, Fairview High School, graduated between 60 and 70 students each year. My sophomore year, 1975, we won the regional tournament which gave us a berth to the Kentucky state tournament, known as "The Sweet Sixteen" (the sixteen winners of the sixteen regions in Kentucky). When we walked into Freedom Hall in Louisville, our mouths dropped and we never recovered. In fact, our coach was as nervous as we were.

In the Hoosier film, this wise coach senses their intimidation. He tells one of the players to take a tape measure and mark the distance from the basket to the free throw line. "What's the distance?" he inquires. The player calls out, "Fifteen feet." Next, he tells the shortest player on the team to climb on the shoulders of the tallest player and measure the height of the basket. "How high is it?" he asks. He says, "ten feet." The coach says to the team, "I believe you'll find these are the exact same measurements as our gym back in Hickory."[22] What was the coach doing? He was putting things in perspective. And by putting things in perspective, he reduced their fear. Fear leads to anxiety and an athlete will not normally perform well riddled by fear and anxiety. The same is true for the spiritual life. Fear and anxiety can overwhelm faith.

There is nothing in the story to suggest that Peter had any doubts about the adequacy and power of Jesus. His faith in Jesus did not waver. It took a robust faith in Jesus for Peter to say, "Lord, if it is you, command that I come to you on the water," and then to actually get out of the boat when Jesus said, "Come." Peter did not doubt Jesus' capacity to overcome the storm; he doubted his own capacity to do so. Peter didn't lack faith *in* Jesus; he lacked the faith *of* Jesus.

Most Christians today equate faith in Jesus with faith in God. When Christians confess that Jesus is Lord, it is natural for them to see Jesus as the functional equivalent of God. Some Christians, however, lose all perspective on what is important by focusing their attention on beliefs about Jesus. For them, believing in Jesus involves believing certain

---

22. *Hoosiers*, Hemdale Film Corporation, 1986.

propositions and theological dogmas about Jesus. Many are even willing to sacrifice the love and compassion of Christ on the altar of their beliefs; that is, it is more important for them to get their beliefs right (correct) than it is to love God, love others, and be faithful disciples of Jesus.

In the Synoptic Gospels, Jesus shows little interest in getting people to believe certain things about him. At an important juncture in his life and ministry, however, he does ask the Twelve what they believe about him. When Peter, representing the Twelve, confesses Jesus to be the Messiah, Jesus says, "Don't tell anyone" (see Mark 8:29–30).[23] Jesus did not want to spark aspirations for a revolutionary, militaristic, royal Messiah who would employ violence to upstage the Romans and set up God's rule. Jesus had no problem accepting his Messianic status (see Mark 14:61–62), but Jesus did not expound a particular doctrine about himself. He proclaimed the good news of God's nonviolent, peaceable kingdom and taught his followers to make the kingdom a priority. Jesus was primarily interested in spreading the kind of faith he himself possessed by awakening this faith in others. He sought to cultivate an attitude of trust in God and compassion toward others, particularly the poor and the oppressed. He sought a response of faithfulness to God's covenant, issuing forth in love for God and love for neighbor. Jesus was the initiator, the catalyst, the lure for a contagious, healing, transforming faith of the kind that he himself possessed. It was more important to Jesus that people share his faith in the loving, gracious, healing God and participate in God's kingdom, than believe that he was the Messiah.

Jesus' faith—his strong conviction that God is good, that God is with and for all God's children, that God's grace and forgiveness are available to all human beings—awakened this kind of faith in others. But while Jesus helped ignite and fuel this kind of faith, it was, nevertheless, their faith.

In the biblical story of David and Goliath, Israel is frightened and paralyzed by the Philistine Goliath's defiance of Israel's God. From a practical point of view, God doesn't even enter the story until David enters the picture. We might mistakenly conclude that David brings God with him; but no, God was already there, they just didn't know it. As pastoral theologian and spiritual writer, Eugene Peterson observes,

---

23. While the charge to silence is more pervasive in Mark's Gospel, it is a theme characteristic of the Synoptic Gospels in general.

David exercised a God dominated imagination. David was immersed in the goodness, largeness, and immediacy of God.[24]

A rather humorous aspect of the story occurs when Saul lends David his armor in preparation for battle with Goliath. It's so big and bulky that David can't move in it. This can be true of anyone who attempts to clothe one's self with someone else's expectations or live off someone else's faith.[25] David needed what was his own. We all do. Other people can mentor us, instruct us, guide us, and council us; they may have wisdom to share and discernment to give that can benefit us greatly, but ultimately when we struggle with Goliath size issues of faith, we must be authentic, real, and true to God and ourselves—we must have our own faith.

The expression in the Gospels that Jesus most often used to identify his role in God's cause (God's kingdom) was "Son of Man." In the Christian tradition, Jesus is the quintessential, representative human being; Jesus reveals to humanity what is possible for humanity. In Matthew 9 Jesus heals a paralytic, but first he forgives him his sins. The healing is secondary; the primary feature focuses on Jesus as the Son of Man exercising the right and power to forgive. Matthew states explicitly that the purpose of the healing was to demonstrate Jesus' authority as Son of Man to forgive sins (9:6). Matthew's conclusion is theological significant, "When the crowds saw it, they were filled with awe, and they glorified God, who had given such authority to human beings" (9:8). They glorified God, not because God had given such authority to Jesus alone, but to human beings. Jesus, as Son of Man, as the representative human being, was exercising the right and authority given to all of us.

When we claim and exercise the power and authority of forgiveness, forgiving others their sins, we are living out our calling as the daughters and sons of God. This is the kind of faith we learn and catch from Jesus, and it is the kind of faith that can enable us to act against our fears.

When Jesus joins his disciples in the boat, the wind and the waves cease. This story, however, is not a story about avoiding storms and the destruction they cause. It was Jesus who sent them out in the boat. As

---

24. Peterson, *Leap Over a Wall*, 39–40.

25. Sometimes, however, we may need the faith of others to get us through a difficult time. In the story of the healing and forgiveness of the paralytic, creatively brought into the presence of Jesus by friends who let him down through the roof of a house where Jesus was staying, Jesus pronounced his sins forgiven when he saw "their" faith (Matt 9:2). Not just the faith of the paralytic, but the faith of his friends as well.

we live in discipleship to Jesus, embodying his faith and compassion, engaging in acts of justice and peacemaking, we can expect to encounter many storms.

In ancient times the sea was regarded as the abode of demons. We too, on our faith voyage, battle demons from within, such as pride, greed, lust, envy, and selfish ambition, as well as demons from without, such as domination systems of injustice and oppression. We struggle to find some balance in our lives—in our management of money, in our relationships, and in our labor and leisure. On the sea in our little boat—tossed about by the wind and the waves, contending with the forces of chaos, battling demons from within and without, wrestling against the principalities and powers set against God's loving, just, and peaceable reign—this is right where we are suppose to be. In fact, one might even argue that we need the storms in order to grow and strengthen our faith. The trees on the edge of the forest that face the full force of the wind are the strongest.

The challenge of faith is not about avoiding storms. Popular author, Nevada Barr tells about the time she and her husband went trekking in Nepal. They traveled with a tour group of eighteen other hikers. At the end of the trip, they spent three days in Chitwan National Park on the border between Nepal and India. On their second day there a naturalist took the group on a guided walk. He herded them slowly through the jungle, pointing out the natural phenomena and explaining each detail. The last of these talks was a dissertation on the track of a tiger found in the tall grasses at the edge of the dirt road they traveled. Something snapped inside her and suddenly she needed to put space between herself and the people she had been jostling elbows with for the past ten days. Slipping away from the outer fringes of the group, she began walking down the road that curled away out of sight in the primeval meadow they were crossing. The naturalist, noticing her escape, began to yell, "Come back. Come back. Don't leave the group. Stay with the group." She pretended not to hear and kept walking. As she rounded the bend out of sight, she could hear him crying, "The tiger will eat you! The tiger will eat you!" Nevada Barr recalls, "At that moment in time I didn't care if the tiger ate me. Better by far to be lunch for a tiger than to spend one more moment in the suffocating crush of the pod."[26]

---

26. Barr, *Seeking Enlightenment Hat by Hat*, 12–13.

Sometimes the tigers will eat us, sometimes they will leave us alone, but there will always be tigers. Faith is not about avoiding the tigers, but walking right into the jungle where they prowl and lurk.

The decision to venture out on the sea where the demonic forces threaten to overwhelm us is not optional. Disciples of Christ have a mission and ministry to the world. We are called to be faithful to our covenant relationship with God—to keep trusting God, loving others, and serving our world, even when shipwreck seems inevitable.

A living faith does not dispel all fear, but it enables us to act against our fear and move forward. It enables us to stay on course and see new possibilities. It compels us to act on the word of Christ, to be faithful to his way and to his call and claim upon our lives. "True faith," says New Testament scholar Eduard Schweizer, is "not the sublime achievement of an especially religious individual, but 'single minded' devotion to the Lord, to his bidding and to his help."[27]

Peter's cry, "Lord, save me" is a legitimate expression of faith. No matter how much faith we possess, we will falter and fail in numerous ways to fully embody God's love. We will have lapses where we regress and digress, but a living faith enables us to still make progress. It keeps us in the race, looking to Christ, the catalyst and pioneer of our faith, who was faithful even unto death on the cross.

---

27. Schweizer, *The Good News According to Matthew*, 323.

2

God's Dream for the World

IN THE MOVIE, *Open Range*, Kevin Costner plays Charlie Waite, a former soldier and gunslinger who works for "Boss" Spearman, a free-range cattleman who is driving a herd cross-country. A conflict ensues between the free-ranging cowboys and a local rancher who wants to take their herd.

Charlie is plagued with guilt on account of the terrible things he did during the war. He falls in love with Sue Barlow, the strong and compassionate assistant and sister of the town's physician. After the final gunfight in which Charlie is wounded, he meets with Sue in the town's shot-up saloon. She says to him, "I don't have the answers, Charlie, but I know that people get confused in this life about what they want, and what they've done, and what they think they should have done because of it. Everything they think they are or did takes hold so hard that it won't let them see what they can be."[1]

There are powerful forces at work in society and in our lives that distort our vision and prevent us from seeing what the world can be and what we can be in it. A living faith enables us to take the blinders off and explore God's dream for the world and our participation in its transformation.

In the Synoptic Gospels, Jesus begins his public ministry after his baptism and temptation in the wilderness. He proclaims God's dream for the world,

> Now after John was arrested, Jesus came to Galilee, proclaiming the good news of God, and saying, "The time is fulfilled, and the kingdom of God has come near; repent, and believe in the good news." Mark 1:14–15

---

1. *Open Range*, Touchstone Pictures, 2003.

This does not mean, "Repent, so you can go to heaven when you die." The "kingdom of God," which in Matthew's Gospel most often appears as "kingdom of heaven," pertains mostly to a transformed earth, a world healed and at peace, sustained by distributive, restorative justice, not another-world reality. Matthew simply follows common Jewish custom by substituting the word "heaven" for "God" out of reverence for God's name. It was popular Jewish practice to avoid common usage of the name of God.

We should not read later, popular notions of "heaven" into Matthew's phrase. New Testament scholar, N. T. Wright has observed that the "medieval pictures of heaven and hell, boosted though not created by Dante's classic work, have exercised a huge influence on Western Christian imagination."[2] Many Western Christians have been brought up or converted into a system of belief that has placed enormous emphasis on the afterlife. Consequently, many Christians simply assume that whenever the New Testament speaks of heaven it refers to the place that the saved will go when they die.

Heaven has a rather diverse and ambiguous history of interpretation among the Jews. In a number of texts in the Hebrew Bible, heaven (or heavens, in Hebrew it is always plural) refers to the canopy covering the earth. In other texts it encompasses all that is above the earth. An ancient worldview that is sometimes reflected in the Scriptures imagined heaven as a dimension of reality corresponding to earthly reality. According to this view, every earthly reality has its heavenly counterpart and vice versa. According to theologian Walter Wink, "this is a symbolic way of saying that every material reality has a spiritual dimension, and every spiritual reality has physical consequences. There can be no event or entity that does not consist, simultaneously, of the visible and the invisible."[3]

During the time of Jesus, many Jews believed in a plurality of heavens or levels of heavenly reality, equating the last level (the third level in some systems, the seventh in others) with Paradise, a holding place for the righteous dead. In Paul's correspondence with the church in Corinth, he refers to a visionary experience or revelation he had, where he was caught up to "the third heaven," which he calls "Paradise," where he heard things that he was not permitted to repeat (2 Cor 12:1–4). This is undoubtedly the meaning of Jesus' words in Luke's Gospel to the dying

2. Wright, *Surprised by Hope*, 18.
3. Wink, *The Powers that Be*, 15.

thief who was crucified beside him. The thief asked Jesus to remember him when he came into his kingdom, and Jesus responded, "Truly I tell you, today you will be with me in Paradise" (Luke 23:42–43). "Paradise" is not to be equated with the kingdom, but it is one aspect or dimension of it. This may be what John's Gospel is referring to when Jesus says, "In my Father's house there are many dwelling places . . . I will come again and will take you to myself" (John 14:1–3). This reality—referred to as the "third heaven," "Paradise," and the "Father's house"—was not the hope or destiny imagined by Jesus when he announced that the kingdom of God/heaven had come near. Yet this seems to be the dominant expectation of most Christians.

A whole mythology has developed around the idea of heaven. Maria Shriver has written a book about heaven (titled *What's Heaven?*) apparently aimed at children, with lots of pictures of fluffy clouds in blue skies. She says that heaven is "a beautiful place where you can sit on soft clouds and talk to other people who are there. At night you can sit next to the stars, which are the brightest of anywhere in the universe."[4] She says that God sends angels down to take you to heaven and from heaven you can watch over your loved ones.

Some of the popular images of heaven developed in hymns, praise songs, and contemporary sermons so lack creativity and imagination that they are hardly worthy of sustained thought. I love the story that Dr. Fred Craddock tells about a girl who asked him a very unusual question about heaven.

He was invited to a church to preach and teach for a few days. A woman said to him, "While you're here, are you going to preach on heaven and hell and judgment and stuff?" Fred said, "Well, I hadn't planned on it. Is that important?" She said, "It is to me and my family."

Fred didn't pay any more attention to it until later that week when the family was leaving the church. An attractive daughter, who was fifteen or sixteen years old, stayed behind to ask him a question. Her question was: "Will I go to hell for not wanting to go to heaven?"

The question caught Fred off guard. He said, "Why in the world are you asking that?" She said, "Well, my mother is real suspicious. Every time I come in she grills me: Where you been? Who was with you? What'd you do? Every time I leave the house: Where are you going? Who are you going with? What are you going to do? When are you going

4. Quoted by Wright, *Surprised by Hope*, 17.

to come home? All the time, very suspicious. The way she gets at me is: If you do this, you won't go to heaven! If you don't do that, you won't go to heaven! All the time: You won't go to heaven! You won't go to heaven! What my mother doesn't understand is that I'm not interested in going to heaven."

Fred was at a loss to know how to respond. He recalled telling his son, "You're grounded!" but he didn't mean it in any kind of ultimate sense.[5] Many Christians look to the church to reinforce their ideas and beliefs about ultimate reality. The problem is that many of these ideas and beliefs have nothing to do with Jesus' vision of God's new world.

Popular ideas that Christians have about heaven were not what Jesus had in mind when he announced the nearness of the kingdom of God. The "kingdom of God" is a dynamic, fluid symbol that has earthly, social, relational, spiritual, and political implications. Most certainly Jesus envisioned a transformed world, not some heavenly or otherworldly reality. Jesus instructed his disciples to pray, "Your kingdom come" (Luke 11:2). Matthew's elaboration clarifies the meaning, "Your will be done, on earth as it is in heaven" (Matt 6:10). The reign of God announced by Jesus had to do with God's will being done *on earth* in the same way that he believed it was being carried out in that dimension of reality called heaven.

The Apostle Paul, who told the Corinthians that being "away from the body" meant being "at home with the Lord" (2 Cor 5:8), did not believe, however, that going home to be with the Lord through death was the goal of redemption. Rather, for Paul, ultimate redemption for individuals and the creation was associated with future resurrection. Paul never tried to explain what the intermediate state between death and resurrection involved, or how it fit into God's overarching plan for the creation. For him, resurrection and participation in God's new creation (the renovation and transformation of the world) was the ultimate hope of those "in Christ" (see 2 Cor 5:17). He wrote to the church at Corinth,

> But in fact Christ has been raised from the dead, the first fruits of those who have died. For since death came through a human being, the resurrection of the dead has also come through a human being; for as all die in Adam, so all will be made alive in Christ. But each in his own order: Christ the first fruits, then at his coming [*parousia*, at the manifestation/revelation of his presence]

---

5. Craddock, *Craddock Stories*, 75.

> those who belong to Christ. Then comes the end [the realization/fulfillment of God's reign on earth] when he hands over the kingdom to God the Father . . . When all things are subjected to him, then the Son himself will also be subjected to the one who put all things in subjection under him, so that God may be all in all. 1 Cor 15:20–28

From Paul's perspective heaven is not the objective. Paul believed that the realization/fulfillment of the kingdom would occur in conjunction with resurrection.

Paul's expression of this hope in his letter to the church in Rome clarifies his belief that all of this relates to this world, not a heavenly other-world. He wrote,

> I consider that the sufferings of this present time are not worth comparing with the glory about to be revealed to us. For the creation waits with eager longing for the revealing of the children of God; for the creation was subjected to futility, not of its own will but by the will of the one who subjected it, in hope that the creation itself will be set free from its bondage to decay and will obtain the freedom of the glory of the children of God. We know that the whole creation had been groaning in labor pains until now; and not only the creation, but we ourselves, who have the first fruits of the Spirit, groan inwardly while we wait for adoption, the redemption of our bodies. Rom 8:18–23

In the passage above, the future redemption of creation and the future redemption of the children of God are inseparably connected and interdependent. In Paul's eschatological scheme of events, when the bodies of the people of God are fully redeemed, that is, when they are resurrected and transformed, all creation will be transformed as well and "will obtain the freedom of the glory of the children of God." Paul envisioned resurrection as a new mode of existence beyond death, but in none of his writings, did he ever suggest that it was intended for a completely different sphere of reality. In whatever way Paul may have imagined this future redemption, he related it to this world. Whether or not this is still a viable expectation for the people of God today may be debated, but what is clear, is that Paul, like Jesus, envisioned a transformed world, not some other-worldly existence.

Jesus' preaching and teaching about the kingdom of God was the central message and theme of his ministry. Matthew's Gospel reads,

> Jesus went throughout Galilee, teaching in their synagogues and proclaiming the good news of the kingdom and curing every disease and every sickness among the people. Matt 4:3

According to the Gospel of Luke, when the disciples confronted Jesus, who had withdrawn from the crowds to a deserted place for prayer and solitude, Jesus said,

> I must proclaim the good news of the kingdom of God to the other cities also; for I was sent for this purpose. So he continued proclaiming the message in the synagogues of Judea. Luke 4:43–44

There is no question that Jesus brought a fresh, new perspective to Jewish kingdom (eschatological) expectation, and the Gospels teach that the redeeming power and reality of God's reign were dynamically present in Jesus' words and deeds. Jesus, however, was a first century Jew and the backdrop for the formulation of his announcement of God's new world was firmly grounded and connected to Israel's hope as proclaimed by Israel's classic prophets, to which we now turn.

THE PROPHETIC VISION

Israel's classic prophets reflected a passion for social justice that was generated from their own experience of the God who entered into covenant with Israel. Their prophetic oracles are peppered with expressions of divine anger and pronouncements of judgment against those in power who took advantage of the poor and oppressed the needy. Consider, for example, the following indictment against the powers that be by the prophet Amos,

> Thus says the Lord: For three transgressions of Israel, and for four, I will not revoke the punishment, because they sell the righteous for silver, and the needy for a pair of sandals—they who trample the head of the poor into the dust of the earth and push the afflicted out of the way . . . Amos 2:6–7a.

In order to avert God's judgment the prophet called upon them to turn from their evil ways and establish justice,

> Seek good and not evil, that you may live: and so the Lord, the God of hosts will be with you. Hate evil and love good, and establish justice in the gate; it may be that the Lord, the God of hosts, will be gracious to the remnant of Joseph. Amos 5:14–15

The prophet went on to declare their worship useless and empty. All their religious festivals and sacrifices were meaningless without restorative, social justice, expressed in love for one's neighbor. The prophet announced,

> I hate, I despise your festivals, and I take no delight in your solemn assemblies. Even though you offer me burnt offerings and grain offerings, I will not accept them; and the offerings of well-being of your fatted animals I will not look upon. Take away from me the noise of your songs; I will not listen to the melody of your harps. But let justice roll down like waters, and righteousness like an ever-flowing stream. Amos 5:21–24

Marcus Borg has observed that by the time the biblical prophets began to address these issues in the eight century, "Israel and Judah had become miniature versions of the ancient domination system that had enslaved them in Egypt."[6] According to Borg, three major features characterize domination systems: a politics of oppression; an economics of exploitation; and a religion that legitimizes the oppressive and exploitive political and economic systems. These prophets, who at times thundered against the injustices of the domination system, put their lives on the line in public protests. Occasionally, they performed rather unusual, attention-getting acts that made for great street theater, as a way of dramatizing their message. For example, Isaiah walked naked and barefoot through the streets of Jerusalem for three years symbolizing what would happen if Israel entered into a military alliance with Egypt against Assyria. Assyria would carry them off naked and barefoot as prisoners of war. Jeremiah shattered a clay jug before the leaders in Judah declaring, "Thus says the Lord, 'So will I break this people and this city.'" Ezekiel laid on his left side for 309 days, then on his right side for 40 days, symbolizing the number of years that Israel and Judah would spend in exile.

When Jesus staged a demonstration in the Temple in Jerusalem, he was acting no different than the classical Hebrew prophets. In Mark's Gospel, Jesus' symbolic action in the Temple is linked to his cursing of the fig tree, another symbolic act. Mark reads,

> On the following day, when they came from Bethany, he was hungry. Seeing in the distance a fig tree in leaf, he went to see

---

6. Borg, *Reading the Bible Again for the First Time*, 127.

> whether perhaps he would find anything on it. When he came to it, he found nothing but leaves, for it was not the season for figs. He said to it, "May no one ever eat fruit from you again." And his disciples heard it.
>
> Then they came to Jerusalem. And he entered the temple and began to drive out those who were selling and those who were buying in the temple, and he overturned the tables of the money changers and the seats of those who sold doves; and he would not allow anyone to carry anything through the temple. He was teaching and saying. "Is it not written, 'My house shall be called a house of prayer for all the nations'? But you have made it a den of robbers." And when the chief priests and the scribes heard it, they kept looking for a way to kill him; for they were afraid of him, because the whole crowd was spellbound by his teaching. And when evening came, Jesus and his disciples went out of the city. Mark 11:12–19

The story of the fig tree, whatever its origin, is intended in Mark's narrative to represent the religious establishment in Israel. In several prophetic texts Israel is portrayed as a fig tree or grape vine without figs or grapes; that is, without the fruit of compassion and justice (see Jer 8:13; Hos 9:10, 16, 17; Joel 1:7; Mic 7:1).

The fig tree incident informs the meaning of Jesus' symbolic demonstration in the Temple. Jesus' action in the temple was not a "temple tantrum" (Borg's phrase); it was a deliberate, intentional, prophetic act. It would have been limited in its effect, disrupting normal temple activity only briefly. Otherwise, the Roman soldiers stationed in the adjacent Fortress Antonia would have intervened. From a Roman imperial point of view, this was a minor disturbance relating to Israel's religion. The Jewish religious leaders, however, were infuriated and determined, more than ever, to get rid of Jesus.

There is some disagreement among biblical scholars as to the exact meaning of Jesus' action, but staged as it was in Israel's religious center, it was certainly a symbolic act depicting God's displeasure with the religious leadership. Jesus' interpretation of his action, according to Mark, combines Isaiah 56:7 and Jeremiah 7:11. The Jeremiah reference was part of Jeremiah's temple sermon. In that oracle, Jeremiah warned Israel that their possession of and worship in the Temple would not save them from God's judgment. Jeremiah warned them not to trust those who were saying, "This is the temple of the Lord" (Jer 7:4)—suggesting that their claim on the temple gave them special protection and grace. Jeremiah called them to repentance, encouraging them with the promise of God's presence,

> For if you truly amend your ways and your doings, if you truly act justly with one another, if you do not oppress the alien, the orphan, and the widow, or shed innocent blood in this place . . . then I will dwell with you in this place, in the land that I gave of old to your ancestors forever and ever. . . . Has this house, which is called by my name, become a den of robbers in your sight? Jer 7:5–7, 11

Marcus Borg has argued that the Hebrew phrase translated "den of robbers" suggests not thievery, but robbing with violence. The temple had become the center of an oppressive system that exploited the poor and powerless. "Their everyday injustice made them robbers, and they thought of the temple as their safe house and place of security."[7] Jesus' action in the temple, then, was not so much a cleansing of the temple as it was an indictment of the religious leadership and activity that centered in the temple.

Whatever the exact nature of Jesus' protest, it was certainly symbolic of God's judgment upon the corruption that apparently was widespread among Israel's religious leaders and their failure to practice distributive justice and compassion. From Mark's perspective this sealed Jesus' fate. Mark says that in the aftermath of Jesus' protest the chief priests and the scribes "kept looking for a way to kill him" (Mark 11:18).

The classical biblical prophets were not only discerning social critics, they also were dreamers of God's dream. While they were not hesitant about naming the sins of injustice and exposing the crimes against the people by the monarchy and aristocracy, they were also heralds of hope, casting an alternative social vision. They poetically and symbolically painted pictures of what the world would be like when God's reign over Israel and the nations is realized. Consider the following vision in Isaiah,

> For I am about to create new heavens and a new earth; the former things shall not be remembered or come to mind. But be glad and rejoice forever in what I am creating; for I am about to create Jerusalem as a joy and its people as a delight. I will rejoice in Jerusalem and delight in my people; no more shall the sound of

---

7. Borg, *Jesus*, 235.

> weeping be heard in it, or the cry of distress. No more shall there be in it an infant that lives but a few days, or an old person who does not live out a lifetime ... They will build houses and inhabit them; they shall plant vineyards and eat their fruit. They shall not build and another inhabit; they shall not plant and another eat; for like the days of a tree shall the days of my people be, and my chosen shall long enjoy the work of their hands. They shall not labor in vain, or bear children for calamity; for they shall be offspring blessed by the Lord—and their descendants as well. Before they call I will answer, while they are yet speaking I will hear. The wolf and the lamb shall feed together, the lion shall eat straw like the ox; but the serpent—its food shall be dust! They shall not hurt or destroy on all my holy mountain, says the Lord. Isa 65:17–25

The prophets envisaged a new world of restorative justice and peace. It was against this backdrop that Jesus announced the good news of God's reign. Jesus infused the concept with a more expansive, flexible, and dynamic meaning (in some passages "kingdom of God" simply functions as an intensive symbol for the healing, transforming power of God), yet his vision was firmly grounded in the eschatological hope of Israel's classic prophets and their portrayal of a new society freed from poverty, oppression, and violence.

Obviously, there are deep inner, spiritual, and personal dimensions to the good news of God reigning in the world. In order to have transformed systems, institutions, and communities, the individuals who constitute and lead them must be transformed. This is why Jesus talked about dying to the ego, about being born anew, about being pure in heart, and about hungering and thirsting after righteousness/justice. The call to repent, in light of the present/coming reign of God, was a call to stop living for self-glory, self-honor, and self-fulfillment, and to live for the good of all humankind and all creation.

GOOD NEWS TO THE POOR

Dr. Wayne Ward taught theology at Southern Baptist Theological Seminary for many years when that school was still a very credible and highly acclaimed institution. In a sermon at Walnut Street Baptist Church in Louisville, Dr. Ward told about the time he learned the truth of Jesus' words, "It is more blessed to give than to receive."

In the summer after his high school graduation, his high school track coach, who was Superintendent of Education in Northeast Arkansas, entered his summer class at Arkansas State College with an urgent plea. He said, "We have an emergency situation. Hundreds of little children in Black River Bottom and in the hills of Crowley's Ridge in the Lemons School District have no one to teach them. The pay is low. Will you help us?" There was a long silence. Finally, Wayne Ward spoke up, "Coach, I'll go." He passed the test that gave him an emergency teaching certificate and off he went to Hickoria School in Black River Bottom.

Wayne Ward fell in love with the mostly poor, ragged, and usually dirty kids that made up his class. They looked to him with yearning eyes to learn and they soaked up his teaching like a sponge. The little boy that touched him most was Eggie Eggenspieler—the most deprived child in the class. He wore the same patched bib overalls and same tattered shirt everyday. He was so skinny Mr. Ward worried over whether he had enough to eat. One day Mr. Ward slipped into the cloakroom and opened his little molasses bucket lunch pail (probably an invasion of privacy), and found one soggy biscuit with mold on it, covered in a sticky gob of molasses. Dr. Ward commented, "Emily Post, in all her etiquette books, never had instructions on how to meet a challenge like that."

Most days of that cold, rainy fall Mr. Ward was out with the kids during recess sloshing through mud and water trying to play kickball or "capture the flag." At lunchtime they opened their paper sacks or molasses buckets, climbed up on the woodpile and gulped down their soggy biscuit sandwiches.

One kid, whose father ran the one country store, had a beautiful lunchbox with a thermos bottle. Mr. Ward often observed the other children looking longingly as Buddy Baker poured out his steaming hot chocolate. Buddy's closest friend was, as one might guess, Eggie. He stuck with Buddy like his shadow. As Christmas approached, Buddy began to have an occasional orange in his lunchbox. Eggie had never seen an orange before. Buddy, sitting on the woodpile, would solemnly peel his orange and hand the peelings to Eggie, who gulped them down like they were some kind of delicacy.

Mr. Ward would silently pray that Buddy would give Eggie one section of a real orange, but he never did. Mr. Ward felt a resolve forming in his heart and decided to see to it that Eggie and all his brothers and sisters got some real oranges for Christmas or he would die trying. On

Friday, before Christmas, as Mr. Ward was dismissing school, he told Eggie that he needed to see him. Eggie turned pale, "What have I done?" he asked. "Nothing," said Mr. Ward, "I'm going home with you." Eggie objected, "You'll get drown-ded!"

Mr. Ward drove down an abandoned railroad "dump," trying to keep out of the flooded bottomland and parked his old "free-wheeling" Plymouth on a built-out siding that railroad handcars had used. When he opened the trunk and began to load Eggie and himself down with bulging sacks of oranges, apples, and toys, Eggie's eyes started to flash like strobe lights. On the first step off the railroad dump they went bobbing for apples. When they got going again Eggie said, "Follow me, Mr. Ward, I know where the high places are" and so he did.

When they got to this little shack that Eggie called home, raised a few feet out of the water, ragged kids came running out to meet them. Inside was a distraught little mother with more kids than she could handle, and there was no father to be seen (he was in prison). Mr. Ward took an orange, broke off a section and insisted Eggie try it. Eggie's face lit up like the sun.

On that Sunday morning when Dr. Wayne Ward shared this story with the congregation he said, "Though I have told this story many times, I still feel a lump in my throat when I remember the miracle of discovering 'it is more blessed to give than to receive' (Acts 20:35) at Christmas or anytime."

But not only did Wayne Ward learn this lesson, Eggie learned it too. Shortly after Christmas, Mr. Ward was asked to referee the junior high basketball games but he didn't have a whistle. One morning when he arrived at school there was a little package on his desk wrapped in paper that had been requisitioned from the wastebasket. As he opened the package he could sense two big blue eyes looking intently at him, waiting for his reaction. Inside was a beautifully carved willow whistle. Mr. Ward shouted, "Beautiful!" and gave the whistle a blow that rattled the windows. Eggie's face lit up the room. You see, he too had learned the wonderful truth that it is more blessed to give than to receive.

After Mr. Ward completed his assignment, it was time for him to go home and start college. As he shifted gears to climb the hill leading out of Black River Bottom, he heard a sound from the floor of his back seat. A mail carrier had recently been jumped and fatally beaten, so Mr. Ward prepared himself. He picked up speed, then suddenly hit the breaks and grabbed for the sound in the back seat. Up popped two big blue eyes. "Eggie!" cried Mr. Ward, "what are you doing in my car?" Eggie said, "I'm going home with you, Mr. Ward. I want you to be my daddy."

Of course, Mr. Ward couldn't take Eggie home. He was going back to college and then into the Navy to serve in World War II. But in the summer of 1939 before he left for college, Mr. Ward was able to get Eggie a job as a scout and runner for the REA (the Rural Electrification Authority), which was running heavy lines and bringing the blessing of electricity to the wilderness of Black River Bottom. Eggie knew the forested bottomland better than the deer and muskrats. The top engineer of REA told Mr. Ward that his eleven-year-old scout and runner was the best "man" he had. Mr. Ward kept in touch with Eggie and when he got back from the war, Eggie was in Arkansas State University. He graduated with a degree in electrical engineering, and when Dr. Wayne Ward told this story in December of 1991 at Walnut Street Baptist Church in Louisville, Eggie was leading the REA program for the northeastern part of Arkansas.[8]

Dr. Wayne Ward's involvement in the life of this needy student is certainly a dramatic example of Christian compassion and generosity. Disciples of Jesus Christ are committed to give generously to alleviate the needs of the poor and impoverished. In 2 Corinthians 8–9, Paul urged the Corinthians to give joyfully, graciously, and generously to the collection he was receiving from churches for the poor disciples in Jerusalem. Paul grounded his appeal on the self-giving of Jesus, "For you know the generous act of our Lord Jesus Christ, that though he was rich, yet for your sakes became poor, so that by his poverty you might become rich" (2 Cor 8:9).

Giving to the needy is a vital characteristic of Christian discipleship, but it is only one side of the coin. Disciples of Jesus must equally be concerned about the economic and political systems of society that create poverty. Christians have a responsibility to be aware of and active in correcting and changing public policy, following Jesus in exercising a preferential option for the equitable treatment of the marginalized and the downtrodden. William Sloan Coffin has stated it well, "Obviously the churches have to feed the hungry, clothe the naked, and shelter the homeless. But they have also to remember that the answer to homeless-

---

8. This story was adapted from a transcript of Dr. Wayne Ward's sermon at Walnut Street Baptist Church in Louisville. I no longer possess the transcript.

ness is homes, not shelters. What the poor and downtrodden need is not piecemeal charity, but justice."[9]

There is a strong tradition in the Hebrew Bible of distributive justice. It is grounded in a theology of creation that asserts, "The earth is the Lord's and all that is in it, the world, and those who live in it; for he has founded it on the seas, and established it on the rivers" (Ps 24:1–2). From this point of view, all property rights and material wealth are relative. Everything belongs to God and we are tenants and stewards who hold everything in trust.

Boundaries and stipulations were built into Israel's covenant with God that made provisions for equitable distribution of land, which was the primary source of wealth in the ancient world. According to these provisions: a) The charging of interest within Israel was forbidden (Deut 22:25; 23:19; 25:35–37). b) Debts were erased every seventh (sabbatical) year. In Israel's agricultural economy debts were mostly charitable loans, since charging interest to other Hebrews was prohibited (Deut 15:1–2). Israel was warned not to refuse charitable loans to the poor even when the Sabbatical was near (Deut 15:10). c) Slaves were released on the sabbatical year. The law applied to both male and female slaves, though with different provisions (Exod 21:7–11; Deut 15:13–14, 18). d) The land was to lie fallow every sabbatical year. Crops were not to be planted nor harvested; the poor, however, were permitted to glean from the plants that came up on their own. e) Every fiftieth year (or year of Jubilee) the land reverted back to its original owner (Lev 25:10). This provided for just and fair distribution of God's land. If people had lost their land through bankruptcy, it was restored to them. These provisions were designed to reduce poverty and circumvent the ever-widening gap that occurs in most economic systems between the wealthy and the poor.

Theologian, Donald B. Kraybill has observed that the whole Jubilee concept was rooted in an awareness of human sin and greed. Constraints were needed to defend the defenseless and protect the helpless. Without these constraints, wealth and power tended to concentrate in the hands of the few. Jubilee legislation was designed to circumvent this concentration of power and wealth and help implement economic justice. Jubilee was not intended to establish economic equality, but it was designed to curb selfish ambition and level pyramids of elite power and wealth. The Jubilean vision was not intended to squelch individual initiatives or

---

9. Coffin, *A Passion for the Possible*, 36.

personal aspirations, but it was grounded in the full awareness that such aspirations could easily get out of hand. So it wisely mandated "structural change at regular intervals to equalize the disparities which would otherwise run rampant."[10] Benevolence could not be left to the personal whims and wishes of the rich. Jubilee integrated the spiritual, social, and economic dimensions of life into one piece.

According to Luke's Gospel, Jesus regarded Isaiah 61:1–2a as an explanation of his kingdom mission. In the synagogue of Nazareth, Jesus read his job description,

> The Spirit of the Lord is upon me, because he has anointed me to bring good news to the poor. He has sent me to proclaim release to the captives and recovery of sight to the blind, to let the oppressed go free, to proclaim the year of the Lord's favor. Luke 4:18–19

With all eyes fastened on him he returned the scroll to the attendant and announced, "Today this scripture has been fulfilled in your hearing" (Luke 4:21). Most interpreters agree that Jesus was not calling for a specific program of social and economic reform, but without question, he was casting a social vision based on the ethics of distributive justice within the Hebrew tradition. His announcement of God's reign was permeated by the spirit of Jubilee and the equitable principles of justice incorporated into Israel's covenant with God.

Against this backdrop, the blessings and woes in Luke 6:20–26 make sense,

> Blessed are you who are poor, for yours is the kingdom of God. Blessed are you who are hungry now, for you will be filled. Blessed are you who weep now, for you will laugh. Blessed are you when people hate you . . . But woe to you who are rich, for you have received your consolation. Woe to you who are full now, for you will be hungry. Woe to you who are laughing now, for you will mourn and weep. Woe to you when all speak well of you . . .

The way the "poor" and "rich" are juxtaposed in this passage may suggest that the rich became wealthy at the expense of the poor.[11] New Testament scholar, Alan Culpepper has pointed out that these blessings and woes speak "to real socioeconomic conditions, not spiritual condi-

---

10. Kraybill, *The Upside-Down Kingdom*, 92.
11. See the story of Lazarus and the rich man in Luke 16:19–31.

tions or attitudes, and they declare God's partisan commitment to the poor and the oppressed."[12]

These words of Jesus were just as radical to those who first heard them as they are to readers today. They overturned conventional wisdom and cut against the grain of popular belief. Many of Jesus' hearers embraced the notion that wealth was the sign of the blessing of God, and certainly one could find justification for that belief in Israel's Scriptures. A common tradition claimed that those obedient to Israel's covenant with God would be blessed with physical and material prosperity (Deut 28). Poverty, then, was regarded as a sign of God's displeasure and judgment. Jesus radically countered such ideas in these pronouncements of blessing and woe.

Luke's portrait of Jesus, announcing a reversal of blessings and woes in the context of God's reign, presents a difficult picture for many modern Christians to accept, especially those who look to Christ primarily for comfort and satisfaction. In the language of Dietrich Bonhoeffer, Luke's Jesus speaks of "costly grace" as opposed to "cheap grace," which offers "justification of sin without justification of the sinner."[13] For many present day Christians, Luke's proclamation of Jesus' message and his depiction of Christian discipleship constitute a Christianity yet to be tried.

Jesus' declarations of blessing and woe serve as a call for repentance—a reordering of values and priorities, especially economic priorities. Luke's Gospel is filled with warnings from Jesus on the dangers of wealth. Wealth tends to foster a spirit of pride and self-sufficiency that closes the door to God's grace. After a rich man refused to give away his possessions in order to become Jesus' disciple, Jesus said, "How hard it is for those who have wealth to enter the kingdom of God! Indeed, it is easier for a camel to go through the eye of a needle than for someone who is rich to enter the kingdom of God" (Luke 18:24–25). New Testament scholar, James D. G. Dunn has presented a theological perspective on wealth and poverty that is worth repeating here,

> The danger of wealth is obviously that it encourages the attitude which is the reverse of that of "the poor"—self reliance (or should we say wealth-reliance) and selfish ambition. The danger of wealth is that it becomes an instrument of power, and so corrupts,

12. Culpepper, *The Gospel of Luke*, 143.
13. Bonhoeffer, *The Cost of Discipleship*, 43.

a means of influencing others and gratifying the self, a reason for adopting a rat-race attitude to life and for trampling others into dust. The danger of wealth is that it encourages a disregard for spiritual values and resources, a trust in one's own strength and in what one controls. The power of poverty is that it discourages trust in one's own resources, facilitates a disengagement from the values of this world, and points to God as the measure of and means to lasting value. The poverty of wealth is that it makes it hard to distance one's true self from materialistic values, to disengage from attitudes which measure success by financial return, to recognize the character of the riches available to the human spirit. As material poverty so often goes hand in hand with an awareness of dependence on God (the poor), so material wealth too often goes hand in hand with pride and the selfish exercise of the worldly power which wealth usually brings.

Here too is an uncomfortable emphasis in Jesus' teaching too often ignored, and not least by members of today's rich First World. The good news for the poor is bad news for the rich! God's blessings are for beggars! They are for those who, whatever their circumstances in life, know that before God they are only beggars! Although Jesus refused the option of political revolution, his message and life-style had revolutionary consequences . . .[14]

When we serve the poor we are serving Christ. In one of the judgment parables in Matthew, the criterion for judgment involves mercy given or withheld from the poor, sick, hungry, and destitute (Matt 25:31–46). To those who extended compassion and help to the downtrodden Jesus says, "Truly I tell you, just as you did it to one of the least of these who are members of my family, you did it to me" (Matt 25:40). This text suggests that Jesus enjoys a special connection and solidarity with "the least" of his brothers and sisters (least from the world's perspective, not Jesus'). These are "the last" who in the reversal of God's reign will be "the first."

Disciples of Jesus share Jesus' prejudicial regard for the poor, the disadvantaged, and those demoted and disregarded by people of position and power, by acting compassionately and giving generously to alleviate their needs, and by engaging and confronting the societal systems that help create and perpetuate poverty.

---

14. Dunn, *Jesus' Call to Discipleship*, 57–58.

GOD'S UNCONDITIONAL LOVE

A story is told about Dr. John Mackie when he was president of the Church of Scotland. Sometime after World War II, during the reconstruction of Europe, the World Council of Churches wanted to see how its money was being spent in some remote parts of the Balkan Peninsula. It dispatched Dr. John Mackie, along with two other ministers, both strong conservatives. One afternoon Dr. Mackie and the two other clergymen went to call on the Orthodox priest in a small Greek village. The priest was overjoyed to see them and was eager to pay respects.

Immediately, he produced a box of Havana cigars, a great treasure in those days, and offered each of his guests a cigar. Dr. Mackie took one, bit the end off, lit it, puffed a few puffs, and said how good it was. The other gentlemen looked horrified and responded very sternly, "No thank you, we don't smoke." Realizing he had somehow offended the two who refused, the priest was anxious to make amends. So he excused himself and then returned a couple of minutes later with a bottle of his choicest wine. Dr. Mackie took a glassful, sniffed it like a connoisseur, sipped it, and praised its quality. His companions drew themselves back even more noticeably than before and responded harshly, "No thank you, we don't drink."

Later when the three men were in the jeep leaving the village, the two clergymen tore in to Dr. Mackie, "Do you mean to tell us that you are president of the Church of Scotland and an official representative of the World Council of Churches and you smoke and drink?" Dr. Mackie retorted, "No, damn it, but somebody had to be a Christian!"

Somebody had to be a Christian; that is, someone had to reflect the gracious, hospitable, welcoming spirit of Christ. Someone had to be not only tolerant, but accepting.

Theologian, Paul Tillich is best remembered for his book, *The Courage to Be*, but his sermons were much more accessible. In perhaps his most famous sermon titled, "You are Accepted," preached on college campuses across the country, he proclaimed,

> You are accepted. You are accepted, accepted by that which is greater than you, and the name of which you do not know. Do not ask for the name now; perhaps you will find it later. Do not try to do anything now; perhaps later you will do much. Do not seek for anything; do not intend anything. Simply accept the fact that you are accepted. If that happens to us, we experience grace.[15]

15. Quoted by Gomes, *The Scandalous Gospel of Jesus*, 238–39.

This lies at the heart of the gospel of Jesus that is dramatically demonstrated and realized in Jesus' table fellowship with sinners. In Mark's Gospel, after Jesus called Levi, a tax collector, to be his disciple, Levi's house served as a gathering place for "many tax collectors and sinners" (Mark 2:15) who came to eat with Jesus. Tax collectors were particularly despised by the religious establishment because of their collaboration with the Roman government in their oppressive tax system. Jewish tax collectors were regarded as traitors by the pious and were disdained for their greed and love of money.

To eat a meal together in that culture implied friendship and acceptance. Jesus' table fellowship with tax collectors and sinners meant that Jesus embraced as friends the most rejected, condemned, and notorious "sinners" of his day. There were laws in the holiness code about this and no "righteous" Jew would mingle and dine with such sinners. Jesus' disregard of the authority of the religious gatekeepers and his acceptance of the very ones they condemned aroused their ire. In response to their complaints and questions Jesus declared, "Those who are well have no need of a physician, but those who are sick; I have come to call not the righteous but sinners" (Mark 2:17). Luke's version adds the words, "to repentance," making repentance a key component in accepting the call to discipleship (Luke 5:32).

Jesus called his followers to repentance; he expected his disciples to reorient their attitudes, priorities, and goals around God's reign. Jesus' first act, however, was to lavish the guilty with grace. Jesus first welcomed sinners, bestowing gifts of forgiveness and acceptance, then he extended the call to repentance. Jesus challenged his disciples to die to their egos, to change the way they think, to reorder their passions and interests, and to live in the power and reality of God's new world. But the call was issued in a context of grace and acceptance, not exclusion or condemnation. Like the father in the parable of the father and his two sons (Luke 15:11–32) and like Jesus, who forgave his executioners while being executed (Luke 23:34), God's love is not conditioned on repentance. God loves the sinner, even when the sinner rejects that love.

God's acceptance is unconditional. I suppose we can debate whether or not the President of the United States or a key representative such as the Secretary of State should meet with other global leaders without preconditions, but God certainly meets with us without preconditions. God doesn't say, "I love you if you believe the right things, if you say the right things, if you do the right things." There is no regulatory list of do's and don'ts that limit God's love for us.

In the movie, *Artificial Intelligence: A.I.*, technologically advanced androids are used and then discarded when they are no longer deemed useful. One android, a child model named David, is adopted by a woman who believes her real son is going to die. When he recovers, David is sent away. David is devastated by this rejection and begins a journey to become a "real" boy, so that his mother will love him. In a conversation with another android named Joe, Joe says to David, "She (his mother) loves what you do for her. She does not love you, David. She cannot love you."[16] How different is God's love. The writer of 1 John expresses it well, "See what great love the Father has lavished on us, that we should be called children of God! And that is what we are!" (1 John 3:1)

In Luke's Gospel there is an intriguing story that highlights the contrast between Jesus' acceptance of sinners and the rejection and condemnation of sinners by the religious leaders (Luke 7:36–50). Simon, a Pharisee, invites Jesus to dinner. Unlike in our culture, this would have been more of a public than private event, with townspeople gathering around the walls inside or the courtyard outside to witness the occasion. A woman present at the dinner intrudes into the very space of Jesus and the Pharisee. This is not just any woman; Luke identifies her as "a woman of the city, who was a sinner"—undoubtedly meaning a prostitute (7:37).

The guests would have been reclining on their left arms, eating with their right hands, with their feet extended away from the table or mat on which the food was placed. The woman, therefore, would have had easy access to Jesus' feet. Luke says that she "brought an alabaster jar of ointment," suggesting that she came prepared to express her gratitude to Jesus by anointing his feet. The impression is that she had previous contact with Jesus and discovered in his presence the gift of forgiveness and acceptance, for she now comes prepared to express her appreciation. The depth of gratitude that overtook her in the act, however, was spontaneous. Luke reads, "She stood behind him at his feet, weeping, and began to bathe his feet with her tears and to dry them with her hair. Then she continued kissing his feet and anointing them with the ointment" (7:38).

Her spontaneous expression of appreciation and gratitude would have been a direct violation of social conventions, and to Simon, the Pharisee, it was scandalous and deeply offensive. Her touching or caress-

---

16. *Artificial Intelligence: A.I.*, Warner Brothers, 2001.

ing Jesus' feet and her letting down her hair to dry them would have had sexual overtones. In addition, she would have been considered "unclean" (ritually and spiritually impure) according to the holiness code of the Pharisees, so for her to touch Jesus in this manner would have rendered Jesus unclean. In their way of thinking, such impurity was contagious. Simon assumes that if Jesus was a prophet he would know what sort of woman it is who is touching him and would not allow it. Of course, Jesus not only knows what kind of woman this is, he also knows the kind of man Simon is and it is on this knowledge that the story quickly turns, revealing Simon to be the one who is spiritually destitute and without spiritual understanding.

Jesus speaks directly to Simon, telling him a story. If a certain patron has two debtors who are unable to pay him, one owing a small amount and the other owing a large amount, and if the patron cancels the debt of each, then who would love him more?

Simon must feel a trap coming because he is somewhat tentative in his response, "I suppose the one for whom he canceled the greater debt." Jesus affirms his response and then proceeds to contrast Simon's lack of hospitality with the woman's outpouring of gratitude. Simon had not even offered Jesus the common gestures of hospitality. He had provided no water with which to wash his feet, no customary kiss, and no oil for anointing his head. By contrast, says Jesus, the woman "bathed my feet with her tears and dried them with her hair . . . has not stopped kissing my feet . . . has anointed my feet with ointment" (7:44–46). Jesus concludes, "Therefore, I tell you, her sins, which were many, have been forgiven; hence she has shown great love. But the one to whom little is forgiven, loves little" (7:47).

This does not mean that Simon only needed a little forgiveness, while the woman needed a lot of forgiveness. The self-righteousness and aura of superiority expressed by Simon were just as sinful (perhaps even more so) as the woman's prostitution. The difference was that Simon didn't realize his need, while the woman did. Simon was too blinded by his smugness and spiritual arrogance to see how much he needed God's grace. He loved little because he knew so little of God's forgiveness; his self-sufficiency and self-righteousness kept him from experiencing God's grace. This was not because God's grace was closed to him. Simon locked the door from the inside, as does anyone who does not know God's grace and acceptance. God's grace is available for the claiming. All one has to do is graciously receive what is graciously given. When we experience God's forgiveness and abundant provision as pure gift, gratitude wells up from within like a spring of living water, showering all who are around us with love and thanksgiving.

The film, *Wit*, is about a single woman's battle with terminal cancer. Vivian Bearing, no longer able to continue her work as an English professor, has to deal with experiential cancer treatments in a struggle for her life. In one scene, Vivian is in her hospital bed so weak and sick that she can hardly move. Her college English teacher, E. M. Ashford comes to visit, takes out a children's book titled, *The Runaway Bunny*, and begins to read, "Once there was a little bunny who wanted to run away. So he said to his mother, 'I'm running away.' 'If you run away,' said the mother, 'I will run after you. For you are my little bunny.' 'If you run after me,' said the little bunny, 'I will become a fish in a trout stream and I will swim away from you.' 'If you become a fish in a trout stream,' said the mother, 'I will become a fisherman and I will fish for you.'"

At this point E. M. turns the page and says, "Oh, look at that. A little allegory of the soul. Wherever it hides, God will find it." Then she shows Vivian the picture of the mother rabbit fishing in a stream—a carrot dangles from the end of the fishing pole. She continues reading, "'If you become a fisherman,' said the little bunny, 'I will be a bird and fly away from you.' 'If you become a bird and fly away from me,' said the mother, 'I will be a tree that you can come home to.' 'Shucks,' said the little bunny. 'I might just as well stay where I am and be your little bunny.' And so he did."[17]

We can live our lives bouncing from relationship to relationship, from experience to experience, constantly looking for "the something" that is already ours. What we are all looking for has already been given. All we need to do is unwrap the gift and claim the forgiveness, love, and acceptance that is already ours.

CALLED TO BE A COMMUNITY OF LOVE

A prominent theme in Paul's letters that is particularly emphasized in his introductory greeting in his letter to the Romans is the idea of "call." Paul identifies himself as a "servant of Jesus Christ, called to be an apostle, set apart for the gospel of God" (Rom 1:1). He identifies the church as a community of faith "called to belong to Jesus Christ . . . God's beloved in

17. *Wit*, HBO films, 2001.

Rome, who are called to be saints" (1:7). I suspect that many Christians might think of someone like Mother Teresa when the word "saint" is used in a religious context. They would think of a saint as an extremely holy, super-spiritual person, a notch above ordinary religious folks. Sainthood, however, is not something to be achieved or earned, a reward for holy living. Like Israel, disciples of Jesus are called to a certain kind of life. They are called to live out Jesus' love and teachings, but disciples do not conform to Christ's teachings in order to become saints. Rather, they follow Christ because they are saints. The basic concept means "set apart ones" and reflects Old Testament usage. Israel was set apart and chosen by God to live in covenant relationship with God and be a blessing to the nations (Gen 12:1–3).

A better translation is the one offered by C. K. Barrett in his commentary on Romans, "by divine call, saints."[18] Today's English Version reads, "called to be his own people." This is who we are. We are God's people, "God's beloved" (1:7), called to live our daily lives on the basis of this relationship and be a blessing to the world.

In the movie, *Family Man*, Jack Campbell (played by Nicolas Cage) is a successful president of an investment house in New York City. He is single and has everything he wants, or so he thinks. One day he wakes up to a "what if?" kind of scenario, finding himself twelve years into marriage with his college sweetheart and with two small children, helping manage his father-in-law's car dealership. At first he desperately tries to recover his old life, but in the process realizes that living life for one's self is not as joyful, fulfilling, or meaningful as living for others. In one scene Jack discusses with his wife a job opportunity that would revive some of his former glory. It would mean a lot more money and responsibility, and he would have more power and clout, but it would also involve a major move for the family. Kate says to Jack, "Maybe I was being naïve, but I believed that we would grow old together in this house. That we'd spend holidays here and have our grandchildren come visit us here. I had this image of us all gray and wrinkly and me working in the garden and you repairing the deck. Things change. If you need this, Jack, if you really need this—I'll take these kids from the life they love, and I'll take myself from the only home we've ever known together, and I'll move wherever you need to go. I'll do that because I love you. I love you. And that's more important to me than our address. I choose us."[19]

18. Barrett, *The Epistle to the Romans*, 22.
19. *The Family Man*, Universal Pictures, 2000.

God says to each person, "I choose you." We are chosen not because of what we can do for God, not for the tasks we can accomplish, but rather, we are chosen simply because we are human, because we each bear the image of God. Our life comes from God and is sustained by God. I am loved as me. You are loved as you. It's not about what we do, achieve, or accomplish, nor is it about rewards and punishments. It's all about grace.

Popular author and speaker, Tony Campolo tells about playing spelling baseball in the sixth grade. The teacher chose Albert and Mary as captains. Mary, says Campolo, was the kind of kid that if the class was required to hand in a book report, hers would stand out above all the others. It would be covered with special colored paper, with drawings and beautiful lettering all over it. The teacher would hold up her report and say, "Isn't Mary wonderful?"

Albert was Tony's best friend and so Tony figured that Albert would choose him first, but he didn't, even after he waved his hand at him and made a big commotion. Tony wasn't a good speller and that was more important than being a friend. Finally, when everyone was chosen, the teacher assigned Tony to Albert's team. Tony was the first out. He misspelled grasshopper; he didn't know it had two p's. When he missed it, the teacher turned to the other team and Mary jumped in quickly with the correct spelling. She spelled it with a certain flare looking straight at Tony. Tony says, "With each letter I felt pain. It was like a knife going in me every time little Mary sounded out one of the letters." Campolo says that he learned two lessons that day. First, success is more important than friendship. And second, Mary's success was built on his failure.[20]

The world often makes value judgments based on the criteria of affluence, appearance, and accomplishment. Competition drives the system. But God's choice is grounded in grace and has nothing to do with merits earned or rewards won. God loves unconditionally. God does not shout this message; God speaks in a still, small voice. If we give time and attention to the boisterous, fearful, demeaning voices in our culture that exclude and condemn based on conventional expectations, then we can easily become victims driven in either of two directions. On the one hand, we may find ourselves puffed up with pride, thinking ourselves better than others. On the other hand, we may cower in self-contempt, regarding our selves as the scum of the earth. An inflated ego or a deflated ego results from listening to the voices of power that are pervasive

---

20. Campolo, *Let Me Tell You a Story*, 179–181.

in the systems and structures of our world, rather than listening to God's Spirit. These voices try to convince us that we must prove that we are worthy of love.

A little boy was trying to learn the Lord's Prayer that was part of the worship liturgy each Sunday. The congregation always said the Lord's Prayer together and he had been listening quite intently so that he could participate. One Sunday as the congregation was praying he could be overheard saying, "Our Father who art in heaven, I know you know my name." I like his version. God knows our names. God has named us before anyone else has.

This core truth of our existence—that we are loved and chosen by God—does not mean that others are rejected. This is one of the key dynamics of an inclusive gospel: All are chosen! We tend to think in terms of selection and rejection, inclusion and exclusion; if some are chosen then others are passed over. But with God, it's not a matter of being in or out. We are all members of God's family. It's a matter of claiming our unique place and living in light of God's love and call upon our lives. No one else can live my life or your life, though each life is not meant to be lived alone.

Each life is one of a kind intended to be part of a special community—a community of love. The primary human goal of the kingdom of God is about the formation of God's Beloved Community. Living as God's Beloved Community includes sharing what we have with others, forgiving one another, and nurturing open, honest, and redemptive relationships within and outside our communities of faith.

The kingdom of God is by no means limited to our faith communities, but our faith communities have key roles in nurturing kingdom people. Quaker educator and author, Parker Palmer has written about the guidance, encouragement, and support such a community can provide. They offer us unconditional love, refusing to judge our deficiencies or to force change upon on. They provide a safe place for us to develop as human beings, surrounding us "with a charged force field that makes us want to grow from the inside—a force field that is safe enough to take the risks and endure the failures that growth requires."[21] A loving community helps us to accept and endure our failures, while inspiring us to take the risks that love demands. Palmer spoke of the importance of developing circles of trust which combine unconditional love with hopeful expectancy. He observed that in such a space "we are freed to

---

21. Palmer, *A Hidden Wholeness*, 60.

hear our own truth, touch what brings us joy, become self-critical about our faults, and take risky steps toward change—knowing that we will be accepted no matter what the outcome."[22]

Palmer told about facilitating a group of some twenty elected and appointed officials from Washington, D.C. All of them had gone into government work animated by the ethic of public service and all were experiencing painful conflicts between their values and power politics. One participant had worked for a decade in the U.S. Department of Agriculture after farming for 25 years in northeastern Iowa. On his desk at that moment was a proposal related to the preservation of midwestern topsoil, which was being depleted at a rapid rate by agribusiness practices that valued short-term profits over the well-being of the earth. His "farmer's heart" knew how the proposal should be handled, but his political instincts warned him that following his heart would result in serious trouble, beginning with his immediate superior.

On the last morning of the gathering, looking bleary-eyed, he told the group that it had become clear to him during a sleepless night that he needed to return to his office and follow his "farmer's heart." Someone asked him how he would deal with his boss and he replied that it wouldn't be easy. Then he said, "But during this retreat, I've remembered something important: I don't report to my boss. I report to the land."[23] The breakthrough came in a loving, accepting, caring community that gave him the freedom and encouragement to be true to himself. If the people on that retreat had tried to use him to get leverage on public policy, it is not likely he would have heard his soul say, "You report to the land." If he had been treated as a means to other people's political ends, he would have responded from his intellect, emotions, or ego, but his true self would have been stifled. A community of love genuinely seeks the good of all in that community—they do not try to use each other to advance their own agenda.

THE BODY OF CHRIST IN THE WORLD

A preacher pounded the pulpit and thundered to the congregation, "Is everyone here a Baptist?" A man several rows back answered, "No! I'm a Methodist!" The preacher inquired, "Why are you a Methodist?" He said, "Well, my mother was a Methodist and my father was a Methodist." The

---

22. Ibid., 60.
23. Ibid., 18–19.

preacher retorted, "That's the dumbest thing I have ever heard. If your mother was an ignoramus and your father was an ignoramus, would you be an ignoramus?" "No," said the man, "I suppose I would be a Baptist."

Whatever a church's denominational label and stripe or organizational affiliations, a vibrant, dynamic Christian community is grounded in that community's connection, union, and participation in Christ. An argument could be made from the letters of Paul in the New Testament that possibly the most important foundational theological and social construct on which he based his gospel and founded churches was his understanding of individual and corporate participation "in Christ." This underlies Paul's entire discussion in Romans 6-8 of the disciple's union/identification with Christ in death and Paul's instruction for disciples to walk in the newness of life in the power of the Spirit. It is also the basis of his treatment of Adam and Christ as representative figures of humankind and Christ particularly as the archetype and inaugurator of a new humanity (Rom 5:12-21; 1 Cor 15:20-23, 45-49), which is the key component in God's new creation (Gal 6:15; 2 Cor 5:17). In addition, it is the theological construct out of which Paul proclaims the church to be the body of Christ (1 Cor 12:12-31; Rom 12:1-8).

One of the most significant Pauline statements on the theological, social, and practical implications of what it means to be "in Christ"—the new covenant community, the body of Christ—is found in Galatians 3:26-28,

> For in Christ Jesus you are all children of God through faith. As many of you as were baptized into Christ have clothed yourselves with Christ. There is no longer Jew or Greek, there is no longer slave or free, there is no longer male and female; for all of you are one in Christ Jesus.

For Paul, baptism functioned as the covenantal rite—the outward and visible sign—of participation in the body of Christ.

This Magna Charta of Christian community has explosive social and political implications, calling for the abolishment of all barriers between racial, social, and gender groups. "In Christ" a new community is formed that is mutual, egalitarian, and just. Members of this new community are "dead" to the social, religious, and cultural distinctions of the old world order (Gal. 2:19) and joined "in Christ" to constitute a new humanity.

Paul's threefold affirmation of equality corresponds to a number of Jewish formulas in which this threefold distinction was maintained in hierarchical fashion. Paul's declaration may have been modeled on a Greek formula that goes as far back as Thales in the sixth century BCE.[24] He may have been deliberately drawing a contrast of parallels with the inequalities of the ancient world to demonstrate that all differentiation in worth and status between these groups have been eradicated in the body of Christ. Unfortunately, Paul was not always consistent in his application of this new revelation, sometimes preferring custom and convention over the radical implications of all being one "in Christ." The trajectory of his teaching, however, was generally always in the direction of this egalitarian and just social vision.[25]

Paul says that "in Christ" the faith community forms one body analogous to the human body and that just as the human body has many members with diverse and varied functions, so the body of Christ has many members with many different gifts, talents, and capacities for ministry (Rom 12:4–8; 1 Cor 12:4–31). Paul believed it was important that each disciple in the body utilize and exercise his or her gifts, that all members discover their niche in their service to the body and to the world.

A little boy came out of Sunday school sad. His mother, noticing his dejection, asked him what was wrong. He said with a sigh, "God made me all wrong." He explained that the teacher had told his class that God made them with all the right parts to do the right things—with feet to run and a nose to smell. Then he said, "But God made me all wrong—it's my feet that smell and my nose that runs." It is helpful to match our interests, passions, and abilities with our service and ministry to others.

Paul emphasizes the importance of *each* member of the body functioning in a healthy way. If one member of the body does not exercise his or her gifts of service then the whole body suffers. When Bud Wilkinson, former football coach of the University of Oklahoma, retired from coaching football, he toured widely lecturing on the President's physical fitness program. After one lecture a reporter asked him, "Mr. Wilkinson, what is the connection between football and physical fitness?" He replied,

---

24. Bruce, *The Epistle to the Galatians*, 184.

25. The two most oppressive and notorious patriarchal texts often attributed to Paul—1 Cor 14:33–35 and 1 Tim 2:11–15—were not actually written by him. The text in 1 Cor 14 is undoubtedly a scribal interpolation (see Hays, *First Corinthians*, 245–49) and it is not likely that Paul authored First Timothy (see Pregeant, *Engaging the New Testament*, 430–32).

"Absolutely nothing." He went on to explain, "Football involves twenty-two people on the field who desperately need rest, and fifty thousand people in the grandstand who desperately need exercise."[26] Too often the body of Christ functions like a football game—a few people in the game who desperately need rest, and a bunch of other people in the stands who desperately need exercise. Balance in the body is maintained when all participants share in the ministry and mission of Christ.

The church, as a local and practical expression of the new humanity, the "in Christ" community, is intended by Christ, the head of the church, to serve as a visible, collective, corporate demonstration of the grace, love, forgiveness, and acceptance of God. Dr. William James, the famous American psychologist of years back, was asked once to define what he meant by the word "spirituality" that he used in one of his books. He hesitated at first and then remarked that the word was difficult to define, but he could more readily point to a person who illustrated it. The church is called to be a living, dynamic illustration of the magnanimous love of Christ and the Beloved Community that forms the heart of the kingdom of God. Paul, having declared to the church at Rome that disciples are "members one of another" in the body of Christ (Rom 12:5), admonished,

> Let love be genuine; hate what is evil, hold fast to what is good; love one another with mutual affection; outdo one another in showing honor . . . Contribute to the needs of the saints; extend hospitality to strangers.
> Bless those who persecute you; bless and do not curse them. Rejoice with those who rejoice, weep with those who weep. Live in harmony with one another; do not be haughty, but associate with the lowly; do not claim to be wiser than you are. Do not repay anyone evil for evil, but take thought for what is noble in the sight of all. If it is possible, so far as it depends on you, live peaceably with all . . . Do not be overcome by evil, but overcome evil with good. Rom 12:9–10, 13–18, 21

Dr. Fred Craddock told about the time, before he was married, when he served a small church in the Appalachians, located in a little village on Watts Bar Lake between Chattanooga and Knoxville. It was the custom in that church to have a baptismal service in Watts Bar Lake on Easter evening at sundown. The congregation gathered around a fire and after

---

26. Hendricks, *Say It With Love*, 113–14.

the baptisms they would share a meal together. They had constructed with hanging blankets temporary booths for changing clothes. After the new members were baptized and after they changed their clothes, they gathered around the fire with the rest. Last of all, Fred joined them.

When all were gathered around the fire, Glenn Hickey introduced the new people, giving their names and where they lived and worked. Then they formed a circle around them and each person in the circle gave his or her name and said, "My name is . . . and if you ever need somebody to do washing and ironing . . ."; "My name is . . . and if you ever need anybody to chop wood . . ."; "My name is . . . and if you ever need someone to baby-sit . . ."; "My name is . . . and if you ever need someone to repair your house . . ."; "My name is . . . and if you ever need anybody to sit with the sick . . ."; "My name is . . . and if you ever need a car to go to town . . ."; and so it went all the way around the circle.

After the meal they had a square dance. And then at a time they all knew, Percy Miller, with thumbs in his bibbed overalls, would stand up and say, "Time to go," and everybody left. Percy lingered behind and, with his big shoe, kicked sand over the dying fire. At Fred's first experience of all this, Percy saw Fred standing there taking it all in. He said to Fred, "Craddock, folks don't ever get any closer than this." Craddock concluded the story, "In that little community, they have a name for that. I've heard it in other communities too. In that community, their name for that is 'church.' They call that 'church.'"[27]

The Spirit of the living Christ pervades all creation, but in a particular sense Christ's Spirit permeates the corporate church body and abides with individual disciples who are bound by the new covenant sealed through Christ's death (Rom 8:1, 9). The work of the Spirit in the corporate body and in individual members of the body includes that of revealing, manifesting, and mediating the power and presence of the living Christ.

John's Gospel has a highly developed theology of incarnation that is expressed through the historical Christ, though the incarnation as developed by John does not end with the death of Jesus. Jesus informed the disciples that he would not leave them as orphans, but would come to them (14:18). The primary way Jesus comes to them is in and through the Paraclete,

---

27. Craddock, *Craddock Stories*, 151.

> And I will ask the Father, and he will give you another Advocate [Paraclete], to be with you forever. This is the Spirit of truth, whom the world [the evil domination system set against the truth, love, and justice of God] cannot receive, because it neither sees him nor knows him. You know him, because he abides with you, and shall be in you. John 14:16–17

The one John calls "another Paraclete" functions as "another Jesus." Since the Paraclete comes only after Jesus departs, the Paraclete functions as the presence of Jesus after Jesus is visibly and physically absent. Jesus' promises to dwell within his disciples and in their community are fulfilled in the gift of the Paraclete. This is what Jesus means when, in light of the announcement of his departure, he says, "I will not leave you as orphans; I will come to you" (John 14:18, NIV).

In the theology of John's Gospel, the Paraclete is the continuing presence of Jesus with his disciples. The late and brilliant Johannine scholar, Dr. R. E. Brown, after a thorough analysis of the Johannine passages dealing with the Spirit, concluded,

> The Spirit of Truth is a Paraclete precisely because he carries on the earthly work of Jesus. The Paraclete/Spirit will differ from Jesus the Paraclete in that the Spirit is not corporeally visible and his presence will only be by indwelling in the disciples. The OT theme of "God with us" (the Immanuel of Isa vii 14) is now to be realized in the Paraclete/Spirit who remains with the disciples forever.[28]

According to John's Gospel the continuing work of incarnation—visibly illuminating and revealing the presence and character of God—is now carried on through the Spirit of Christ living in Christ's disciples personally and corporately.

The personal/individual indwelling and the communal/corporate indwelling of Christ through the Spirit must never be severed; they are indivisible threads of the same fabric. The imagery of the vine and the branches that John developed in John 15 holds these two strands inseparably together. This image of the vine and the branches is an image of communal life that stresses interrelationship and mutuality in contrast to the highly prized privatism and independence valued in our Western culture. To be a branch in the vine is to be part of an organic community shaped by the love of Christ. The "much fruit" (15:5, 8) that disciples of Christ bear is their love for one another (15:9–13).

28. Brown, *The Gospel According to John XIII–XXI*, 644.

The church, as the body of Christ and as a community in whom the Spirit of Christ dwells, functions as the incarnational presence of Christ in the world. The Rev Thomas Tewell told about an incarnational encounter he had as pastor of Fifth Avenue Presbyterian Church in New York City at a Christmas Eve service. People had started to gather early that evening for the eleven o'clock service. Among them was a recovering alcoholic, six months sober. This was his first Christmas since having lost his family due to his alcoholism. A family of four that reminded him of his own family sat down immediately in front of him. Seeing this family together was crushing, so he decided he couldn't handle it and needed a drink. As he was leaving the sanctuary, he ran into Rev. Tewell who asked him where he was going. He said, "Oh, I'm just going out for a Scotch." "Jim, you can't do that," Rev. Tewell responded. He knew he was a recovering alcoholic. Rev. Tewell asked, "Is your sponsor available?" He said, "It's Christmas Eve. My sponsor is in Minnesota. There's nobody who can help me. I just came tonight for a word of hope, and I ended up sitting behind this family that reminded me that if I had my life together, my wife and kids would be here too."

Pastor Tewell took his friend into the vestry to talk with a couple of other pastors. Then he went into the sanctuary to welcome the crowd. In his welcome he said, "I have one final announcement. If anyone here tonight is a friend of Bill Wilson—and if you are, you'll know it—could you step out for a moment and meet me in the vestry?" [Bill Wilson was one of the cofounders of Alcoholics Anonymous.] From all over the sanctuary, men and women, and even some college students arose and made their way out. Rev. Tewell remarked, "And there while I was preaching in the sanctuary about incarnation, the Word was becoming flesh in the vestry."[29]

The church incarnates in its life together the grace, love, forgiveness, and acceptance of Christ. The church also incarnates the love of God for the world in its ministry to those in need, its identification with the oppressed, and its work for equitable, restorative justice. In John 20, the resurrected Christ, after greeting his disciples with peace, said to them, "As the Father has sent me, so I send you." Then he breathed on them, says John, and declared, "Receive the Holy Spirit" (John 20:21–22). Jesus' disciples, filled and empowered by Christ's Spirit, continue his mission in the world. This mission of spreading God's love, as I have discussed previously, is as much about standing against the principalities and powers

---

29. Tewell, Preaching Today tape, 247.

in their oppression of the poor and marginalized as it is about extending mercy through acts of kindness and generosity. William Sloan Coffin reminds us, "Compassion and justice are companions, not choices."[30]

The late Clarence Jordan, the founder of Koinonia Farm, an interracial community in Americus Georgia, talked about being invited to speak in a Southern Baptist Church in North Carolina during the civil rights era. He figured it was some swank, aristocratic, liberal church that wanted somebody to come pat it on the back for its liberal views toward race. He figured he would whip up a sermon to hold the church over the brink and singe their eyebrows. He had been a little bitter toward the Southern Baptists ever since they had turned him out five years previously.

To his surprise, it was a little mill-town church that was on the edge of the city and the city had grown up and engulfed it. The church building was probably designed to seat about three hundred, but that day it held about six hundred. What amazed Clarence was that the white and black congregants sat anywhere they wanted to sit. The choir was a combined choir of whites and African Americans. He had to change his sermon subject.

After the worship service, they had dinner on the grounds and once again the people sat anywhere they wanted. They didn't go out to the back yard of the church, they went out on the front yard and spread their tables directly in front of main street and started eating together. Clarence realized that they had been doing this for a long time.

Clarence asked this country pastor, "Were you integrated before the Supreme Court decision?" The pastor responded, "What decision?"

The pastor explained, "Well, back during the depression, I was a worker here in this little mill. I didn't have any education. I couldn't even read and write. I got somebody to read the Bible to me, and I was moved and I gave my heart to the Lord and later, I felt the call of the Lord to preach. This little church here was too poor to have a preacher and I just volunteered. They accepted me and I started preaching. Someone read to me in there where God is no respecter of persons, and I preached that."

Clarence said, "Yeah. How did you get along"? "Well," he said, "the deacons came around to me after that sermon and said, 'Now, brother pastor, we not only don't let a nigger spend the night in this town, we don't even let them pass through. Now, we don't want that kind of preaching you're giving us.'"

30. Coffin, *Credo*, 51.

Clarence said, "What did you do?" "Well," he said, "I fired them deacons."

"How come they didn't fire you?" "Well," he said, "they never had hired me. I just volunteered."

"Did you have any more trouble with them?" "Yeah. They came back at me again."

"What did you do with them that time?" "I turned them out. I told them anybody that didn't know any more about the gospel of Jesus than that, not only shouldn't be an officer in the church, he shouldn't be a member of it. I had to put them out."

Clarence said, "Did you have to put anybody else out?" "Well, I preached awfully hard, and I finally preached them down to two. But those two were committed. I made sure that any time after that, anybody who came into my church understood that they were giving their life to Jesus Christ and they were going to have to be serious about it. What you see here is a result of that."[31]

Why is it that so many Christians and churches, instead of leading the way in the struggle against injustice, stand in the way, either by directly opposing issues of justice or by going mute and saying or doing nothing? Think of how many Christians supported segregation and the Jim Crow laws. It took Southern Baptists an entire century to finally repent of their participation in and support of slavery. Why, still today, do so many Christians stand against basic civil rights for homosexual couples, reject women in pastoral leadership, and typically oppose legislation that would lessen the disparity between the wealthy and the poor? How can that be when the good news of Jesus is not just about a social ethic, but is a social ethic?

LIVING INTO THE FUTURE

The body of Christ indwelt by the Spirit signifies a people of the future living in the present world. Jesus proclaimed the kingdom of God as both a present and future reality. In one sense, God's reign was embodied and manifested in the life, words, deeds, death, and resurrection of Jesus. Jesus' reliance on the power of the Spirit to heal the diseased and the demonized is interpreted in the Synoptic Gospels as God's dominion over evil and death breaking into the present world (Matt 12:28; Luke 11:20). Paul regarded individual and corporate participation in the Spirit

31. Jordan, *The Substance of Faith*, 44–45.

of Christ to mean present participation in the future age of resurrection and the new creation.

According to Paul, the Spirit is given to the church as a "first installment" (*arrabon*) or as "a deposit, guaranteeing what is to come" (2 Cor 1;22, TNIV; also 2 Cor 5:5; Eph 1:14)). The Spirit's active presence in the church functions both as a pledge of things to come and the first installment of God's peaceable kingdom. This same idea is conveyed by the image of "first fruits" coming from the harvest—"and not only the creation, but we ourselves, who have the first fruits of the Spirit, groan inwardly while we wait for adoption, the redemption of our bodies" (Rom 8:23). This all points to the reality that the divine/human transformative, healing power that characterizes God's reign is present in the world, but not in any final or complete sense. Pauline scholar, John Ziesler has put it succinctly, "To live in the Spirit is thus partly to live in the present enjoyment of a future inheritance and also to have the assurance of its coming fullness. The church is then the community of the future."[32]

Participation in and collaboration with the Spirit in working for and manifesting God's new world now, calls for a renunciation of old world values, attitudes, behaviors, strategies, and policies, and faithful commitment to the way of Jesus—the way of selfless service, compassion, humility, justice, and suffering love.

In Mark's Gospel Jesus declares, "The time is fulfilled, and the kingdom of God has come near; repent, and believe in the good news" (Mark 1:15). Jesus is saying, "God's new world is even now breaking into this world where evil holds sway. Reorder your lives. Renounce your love for the things of this world, so that you can experience and participate in God's new world. Live into the future. Trust the good news. A new world is coming. Live it now!"

For Paul, baptism, in addition to serving as the initial covenant rite symbolizing membership in Christ's body, also symbolizes the disciple's union with and participation in Christ's death (Rom 6:1–4). Identification with Christ in death results in deliverance from the power and influence of the old world and incorporation into the new experience of the power (Spirit) of the new creation (God's new world). On this basis Paul admonished, "consider yourselves dead to sin [the enslaving power that characterizes the old world where evil dominates], and alive to God in Christ Jesus" (Rom 6:11)—alive to live as partners, co-

---

32. John Ziesler, *Pauline Christianity*, 70.

workers, and friends of Christ, embodying the conversation, character, and conduct characteristic of God's new world. Paul personalized this in his letter to the Galatians, declaring that "the world has been crucified to me, and I to the world" (Gal 6:14). Through participation in Christ's death, Paul (as is true of all disciples of Christ) died to the power, influence, control, and manipulation of the present evil age, in order to live in the power of "the new creation" (Gal 6:15) through the "law [power] of the Spirit of life in Christ Jesus" (Rom 8:2).

Paul expressed the conflict between the present evil world and the inbreaking of God's new world as a clash between Spirit and flesh,

> Live by the Spirit, I say, and do not gratify the desires of the flesh. For what the flesh desires is opposed to the Spirit, and what the Spirit desires is opposed to the flesh: for these are opposed to each other . . . Now the works of the flesh are obvious: fornication, impurity, licentiousness, idolatry, sorcery, enmities, strife, jealousy, anger, quarrels, dissensions, factions, envy, drunkenness, carousing, and things like these. I am warning you, as I warned you before: those who do such things will not inherit the kingdom of God.
>
> By contrast, the fruit of the Spirit is love, joy, peace, patience, kindness, generosity, faithfulness, gentleness, and self-control. . . . And those who belong to Christ Jesus have crucified the flesh with its passions and desires. If we live by the Spirit, let us also be guided by the Spirit. Let us not become conceited, competing against one another, envying one another. Gal 5:16–26

The conflict between flesh and Spirit is not a conflict between the material and immaterial, or between the spiritual and the physical. The physical/material/body dimension and the inner/immaterial/soul-spirit dimension are both spiritual, both are of God. Paul's use of the term "flesh" is not a reference to the human body. Rather, the Spirit (God's/Christ's active presence) is the power of God's new world; whereas the "flesh" represents the power of the present evil age as it operates in the context of an individual life. Bible translations that render "flesh" as "sinful nature" miss the real significance of the contrast/conflict Paul describes and they leave the impression that the Christian possesses two natures. The "flesh" is the total person operating and functioning under the power of the evil domination system. The "flesh" is the person oriented toward the ego desires of power, honor, control, and greed. The "works of the flesh" demean and destroy; whereas the "fruit of the Spirit" builds up and brings healing to individuals and communities.

The Spirit that brought creative order and beauty out of chaos, the Spirit that raised up prophets to proclaim God's good, merciful, and just purpose, the Spirit that empowered the words and deeds of Jesus and his self-giving unto death on a cross, is the same Spirit that compels us to resist the greed, arrogance, and selfish ambition of the flesh and to confront the militarism, sexism, racism, classism, and all the other "isms" of this evil age that dehumanize, demoralize, and devastate lives, families, and societies. The Spirit inspires and empowers attitudes and actions that serve the good of humankind and demonstrate the goodness of God's new world.

There are strong cultural forces entrenched within the systems and structures of society (principalities and powers) that press all people to conform to the status quo of the present age. Followers of Christ are not exempt from this pressure, but "in Christ" they have been given the authority and spiritual power to overcome. Paul addressed this when he wrote,

> I appeal to you therefore, brothers and sisters, by the mercies of God, to present your bodies [total selves] as a living sacrifice, holy and acceptable to God, which is your spiritual worship. Do not be conformed to this world, but be transformed by the renewing of your minds, so that you may discern what is the will of God—what is good and acceptable and perfect. Rom 12:1–2

As disciples of Jesus live and walk in the power of the Spirit, they are able to discern the good, acceptable, and whole-making will of God and find the strength to resist the temptation to be squeezed into the mold of the world's values and practices.

In John's Gospel when Jesus stands before Pilate and declares, "My kingdom is not from this world," Jesus is not saying that his kingdom is heavenly, while Pilate's kingdom is earthly. Rather, Jesus is saying that his kingdom partakes of a different reality and is governed by a different power—the power of love. Jesus goes on to say, "If my kingdom were from this world, my followers would be fighting to keep me from being handed over to the Jews. But as it is my kingdom is not from here" (John 18:16). Jesus' kingdom does not partake of the spirit of violence and death. The power of Jesus' kingdom is the power to heal, renew, restore, and recreate; it's about the discovery and development of authentic human existence (eternal life).

How will God's dominion be realized in the future? Will this come about by means of a dramatic, divine intervention of God? Most Christian interpreters assume that the early church believed Christ would return visibly and personally to judge evil and finally fulfill the promise of the future kingdom. It is difficult, however, to actually know how literally they understood the expectation of Christ's "coming" (*parousia*). The basic meaning of the word is "presence." Of course, if someone is absent and later becomes present, then that person has "come back" or "returned." But in one sense, Jesus never left. As we have seen, his Spirit is equivalent to his living presence in the church and in the world. Interpreted in this light, Jesus' "coming" (*parousia*) is not an invasion from the outside, but an unveiling, manifesting, appearing from within.

N. T. Wright has argued that the language of the Son of Man coming in the clouds of heaven, found in several contexts in the Gospels, "denotes exaltation, not return. It is apocalyptic metaphor, signifying the vindication of God's people after their suffering."[33] Wright's interpretation, however, may require more of an exegetical stretch than most interpreters are willing to make, but I do agree with his following assessment,

> It is misleading to see this in terms of Jesus "returning" to our world as a kind of space invader coming to sort out a rebel planet. Rather, when God finally ushers in his new creation Jesus will be, in person, both the standard and the instrument of that just and deeply welcome judgment and restoration.[34]

The early Christians adopted the Jewish language of God's return to Zion to judge and save and applied it to Christ. These texts can be applied in a contemporary sense to mean that Jesus, who is already here, will manifest his presence as the central agent in the creation of the new world. Even if the early Christians (oriented as they were around a cosmology of a flat earth under a heavenly dome) understood this literally, there is no reason why the church today needs to maintain the belief that Jesus will descend from another world to earth to usher in the kingdom supernaturally. It seems more likely that God's reign will be implemented through the power of the Spirit working in conjunction and collaboration with Christ's agents and emissaries of justice and peace in the world. The more likely scenario for the realization of God's new

33. Borg and Wright, *The Meaning of Jesus*, 197.
34. Ibid., 201.

world is to be found in the dynamic process of the Spirit, empowering and energizing disciples of Christ (the church) and others, regardless of religious tradition or belief, to confront the powers that be and to engage the world through suffering love, compassionate justice, and nonviolent peacemaking.

It is a legitimate question to ask whether or not the realization of God's new world, as envisaged by Jesus and his early followers, is actually possible. There is no doubt that humanity has evolved in its cumulative spiritual consciousness, inspiring visions of a more compassionate, inclusive, just, and egalitarian world. And yet there are powerfully destructive and evil forces set against the fulfillment of God's new world. Is the vision of God's new world on earth a real possibility? Or is it just a "wish upon a star" with little real hope of actuality?

There are moments when I experience this hope as a genuine possibility; other times, though, it seems more like an unrealistic wish. I am convinced, however, that nothing we do for the redemption of our world—no kindness, no act of forgiveness, no loving word or deed—will be lost; that God's vindication/resurrection of Jesus, who embodied God's new world, is God's pledge that life will overcome the malignant powers of death.

The church is called to bear witness to the redemptive hope engendered through the life, death, and resurrection of Jesus. Whatever the ultimate outcome of our planet, the church is called to be a kingdom community in the present world, functioning as "salt" and "light" (Matt 5: 13-16)—revealing the character of God's future kingdom and preserving what is good, just, and right. Disciples of Jesus devote spirit, mind, and body to the kingdom's fulfillment, engaging imagination, emotions, and physical prowess in the service of God's new world on earth.

In the movie, *As Good as It Gets*, Melvin Udall (played by Jack Nicholson) is a successful writer who is crude, rude, and obsessive-compulsive. He becomes enamored with Carol Connelly (Helen Hunt), a waitress and single mom who is distraught by the health problems of her young son. This unlikely pair begin dating—sort of. In a scene toward the end of the story, Carol meets Melvin at an upscale restaurant. Carol arrives first and is ill-at-ease as she waits for Melvin to arrive. Carol has on a simple dress, while the other patrons are luxuriously attired. When Melvin arrives they require him to wear a dress coat. Refusing to put on a coat furnished by the restaurant, he leaves to purchase one. Meanwhile,

Carol waits unaware of Melvin's plight. When Melvin finally arrives and is seated with Carol, he complains that the management required him to purchase a new coat, while they let her in wearing a house dress. Carol is devastated by the comment and gets up to leave. Melvin, immediately realizing his insensitivity and hurtful remark, begs Carol to stay. She looks at him and says, "Pay me a compliment, Melvin. I need one now." He replies, "I've got a compliment." This deeply flawed and neurotic man says, "Carol, you make me want to be a better man." The comment takes Carol by total surprise, defusing her anger.[35]

The church is called to have a similar function in the world, namely, to make the world want to be a better world. When the church lives by the power of the Spirit and exemplifies the love and compassion of Christ, the church will awaken a thirst and hunger in others for the life the church lives and the love the church incarnates. The church will then be instrumental, in cooperation with the Spirit, in making our world a better world.

Bishop Leontine Kelly was the first African-American woman to be appointed Bishop in the United Methodist Church. Her father was a pastor and she grew up in a parsonage. When she was a little girl, he was assigned to a church in Cincinnati. The community had changed and he was the first African-American assigned to that congregation. The church facilities were magnificent—awe-inspiring Gothic architecture, beautiful polished wood, stained glass windows, and a huge crystal chandelier. Presidents had worshiped in that congregation. Just as impressive was the parsonage. Bishop Kelly says that it was so big that each of the children had his or her own room—something new for them. One day, when her brothers were down in the cellar, they found a hole behind the furnace which seemed to lead to a tunnel. They asked her to go with them to explore it, but she went to get her father instead. They all went down to investigate and when her father saw it he became very excited. Their father took them over to the church cellar and behind the furnace they found some old boards, behind which led to other tunnels.

That night around the dinner table at the Calvary Church parsonage in Cincinnati, her father told them the story of the underground railroad, a railroad that didn't have tracks or trains, but was a network for assisting slaves escape to freedom in Canada. It was against the law to help them and those who were caught were often severely punished,

---

35. *As Good as it Gets*, Columbia Tristar Pictures, 1997.

but the members of the underground railroad accepted the risk. She never forgot what her father said that night, "Children, I want you to remember this day as long as you shall live. We've found a station on the underground railroad. The greatness of this church is not its Gothic architecture, its beautiful furniture, its crystal chandelier. The greatness of this church is below us. We are on hollowed ground. These people dared to risk their lives to become involved and care about the poor, frightened runaway slaves, and that was the mark of their greatness."[36]

The church was not formed to wield power and pursue greatness as the world measures greatness. Rather, the church was created to render unselfish service for the good of others, leading the way in the realization of God's new world. The church was designed to function as an outpost of love, advancing God's peaceable kingdom.

Disciples of Jesus form a new humanity "in Christ." They have died to the values, standards, measurements, and policies of the world that divide, exclude, condemn, alienate, and oppress people. They have been crucified to the attitudes and evaluations that evoke pride and arrogance. What matters to the church is the new creation. As Paul proclaimed, the "new creation is everything!" (Gal 6:15).

BLESSED ARE THE PEACEMAKERS

In Luke's narrative of Jesus' birth the angels proclaim to the shepherds, "Glory to God in the highest, and on earth peace among those whom he favors" (Luke 2:14). Another legitimate way of translating the above phrase is as follows, "on earth peace among all humankind, on whom God's favor rests." God's grace, given to all people, forms the basis for peace. It provides the foundation for the defusing of anger and the letting go of grudges. Without grace there can be no forgiveness and reconciliation.

The angelic announcement referenced above is given to shepherds. For many of us, shepherding evokes a positive, pastoral image. Israel's King David was first a shepherd. But in the first century, shepherds were stereotyped as shiftless, dishonest people who grazed their flocks on other people's land. They were a people mostly despised by the religious establishment in Israel and considered unclean. It is appropriate, then, that this glorious revelation was given to shepherds, because Jesus' min-

---

36. Dunnam, *Exodus*, 54–55.

istry was preeminently a ministry to the poor, the oppressed, the outcasts, the marginalized, the despised, the excluded, and the condemned. In Luke 14 at the great eschatological feast, which is symbolic of the fulfillment of God's rule on earth, the guests at the banquet are the poor, the crippled, the lame, and the blind (14:21).

It was customary in the Roman Empire for poets and orators to announce peace and prosperity at the birth of one who was destined to become emperor. How different, though, is the scene in Luke. The king is born, not in pomp and power, not in a palace among royalty, not in glory and honor, but in a peasant's house and laid to rest in a feeding trough. Angels announce his birth to a few bedraggled shepherds.

Jesus' entry into Jerusalem on a donkey, leading a procession of common people, marks the beginning of Passover week that Christians call Palm Sunday. Each of the Synoptic Gospels includes the scene. It is presented as a deliberate act planned by Jesus. Matthew's version is particularly helpful in expounding its meaning.

Marcus Borg has argued that there were actually two processions that rode into Jerusalem prior to the Passover.[37] About the time Jesus led his procession into the city, the Roman governor, Pilate, would have led a very different kind of procession into Jerusalem. Coming from the west side, from Caesarea Maritima on the Mediterranean coast, Pilate would have entered the city with imperial cavalry and foot soldiers to reinforce the garrison on the Temple Mount. With Jewish expectations running high, it would not have taken much to stir up the more radical zealots and revolutionaries among them.

So from one side of the city comes Pilate with all his pomp and power: soldiers wielding weapons, riding horses, marching in step with golden eagles mounted on poles, their metal and gold armor flashing in the sun. One massive display of military might and power intended to intimidate and curtail any thoughts of uprising against Rome.

From the other side comes Jesus riding on a young donkey: mostly children and the most vulnerable of society, the marginalized and oppressed people of the land, waving palm branches saying, "Hosanna to the Son of David! Blessed is he who comes in the name of the Lord! Hosanna in the highest heaven" (Matt 21:9). The title "Son of David" is a royal title, but what kind of king is this? He rides a donkey in place of a war horse.

37. Borg, *Jesus*, 232.

Matthew says that this took place to fulfill what was spoken through the prophet, "Tell the daughter of Zion, Look, your king is coming to you, humble, and mounted on a donkey, and on a colt, the foal of a donkey" (21:5). This Scripture comes from Zechariah 9:9, though Matthew gives it a new reading. In Zechariah the next verse reads, "He will cut off the chariot from Ephraim and the war horse from Jerusalem: and the battle bow shall be cut off, and he shall command peace to the nations" (Zech 9:10).

What kind of king? What kind of kingdom? God's kingdom (God's new world) is not to be established through military force or power; no violent means will be employed. This is a king that is gentle and humble, typified by his peaceful procession into Jerusalem.

Matthew says that the disciples did as Jesus instructed and "brought the donkey and the colt [two animals], and put their cloaks on them, and he sat on them" (21:7). Matthew offers an interesting twist to the reading by referring to two animals with Jesus sitting on both of them (which is not logical, unless you are Dr. Seuss).

Zechariah only speaks of one animal—"riding on a donkey, that is a colt, the foal of a donkey." The writer employs a common form of Hebrew parallelism—a typical feature of Hebrew poetry. Did Matthew miss the parallelism and misread Zechariah? This would seem unlikely since Matthew and his community were diligent students of Scripture. In Matthew 13, after the section on the parables Jesus says, "Therefore, every scribe who has been trained for the kingdom of heaven is like the master of a household who brings out of his treasure what is new and what is old" (13:52). That's what Matthew is doing here. He is doing something new and strange with an old text in order to show its relevance. Matthew is saying: Don't miss this. This king doesn't ride a war horse. He doesn't come in pomp and pageantry; he wears no armor and bears no weapon. He comes riding a young donkey as a sign of God's peaceable kingdom

In the Sermon on the Mount Jesus gives us a strategy for collaborating with God in the implementation of peace in the world. He says,

> "You have heard that it was said, 'An eye for an eye and a tooth for a tooth.' But I say to you, Do not resist an evil doer. But if anyone strikes you on the right cheek, turn the other also; and if anyone wants to sue you and take your coat, give your cloak as well; and if anyone forces you to go one mile, go also the second mile. Give

to everyone who begs from you, and do not refuse anyone who wants to borrow from you.

"You have heard that it was said, 'You shall love your neighbor and hate your enemy.' But I say to you, Love your enemies and pray for those who persecute you, so that you may be children of your Father in heaven; for he makes his sun rise on the evil and on the good, and sends rain on the righteous and on the unrighteous. For if you love those who love you, what reward do you have? Do not even the tax collectors do the same? And if you greet only your brothers and sisters, what more are you doing than others? Do not even the Gentiles do the same? Be perfect, therefore, as your heavenly Father is perfect. Matt 5:38–48

Whereas the normal human response to violence is either fight or flight, Jesus offers a third way: nonviolent direct action. Theologian, Walter Wink in his book, *Engaging the Powers*, articulates a penetrating exposition of this passage that I draw upon here.[38] Wink points out that the word translated "resist" (*antistenai*) in this context means "to resist violently, to revolt or rebel, to engage in an insurrection."[39] Jesus is not forbidding all resistance, rather he is saying, "Do not react violently to evil, do not counter evil with evil, do not allow violence to cause you to react violently."

In the above text, Jesus presents three examples from his culture of nonviolent direct action. First, Jesus says, "if anyone strikes you on the right cheek, turn the other also." The context here is not a brawl or fistfight where the intent is to harm or injure; rather, this is an example of one who has power and clout using it to humiliate and insult one who does not. To strike the right cheek with the right hand would require a bankhanded slap, which was the usual way for reprimanding inferiors. In the dominant/subordinate structure of the ancient world, this is the sort of humiliating put down that a master might do to a slave, or a husband might do to his wife, or a Roman might do to a Jew.

Jesus is speaking to people who are trapped in an oppressive, hierarchical system of class, race, and gender as a result of imperial occupation. Instead of cowering in submission, Jesus calls for a courageous, nonviolent response. The one stricken stands up straight turning the other cheek toward his opponent, inviting another strike. The one who turns the other cheek is challenging the oppressive behavior of the one who has power. The one stricken refuses to be dehumanized and

38. See Wink, *Engaging the Powers*, 175–193.
39. Ibid., 186.

shamed. In confronting systems of oppression, both Gandhi and King taught noncooperation with anything demeaning and humiliating.

In the second example Jesus imagines a context in which one is being sued in a court of law, "if anyone wants to sue you and take your coat, give him your cloak as well" (see Exod 22:25–27 and Deut 24:10–13). Only a person deeply impoverished would have nothing but a garment to give as collateral for a loan. According to Hebrew law, the garment had to be returned before sunset. Jesus describes a setting where a debtor has sunk deep into poverty and cannot repay his debts, and the creditor has summoned him to court.

Indebtedness was endemic in first century Palestine, primarily as a result of Roman imperial policy. Emperors levied a heavy tax burden on the population. Land was ancestrally owned and passed down over generations, and no peasant would voluntarily relinquish it. Exorbitant interest, however, could be used to drive landowners ever deeper into debt. And debt, coupled with the high taxation of Roman tax policy, could easily pry Galilean peasants loose from their land. As a result, in the time of Jesus large estates were owned by absentee landlords, managed by stewards, and worked by tenant farmers, day laborers, and slaves.

In handing over one's undergarment as well as one's outergarment, the person taken to court would be making a dramatic protest against the system that permitted this kind of oppression. It would have served as a vivid sign of how the oppressors strip the poor of their dignity.

The third example reflects a situation where forced labor was allowed, but limited, "if anyone forces you to go one mile, go also the second mile (5:41). A Roman soldier could force a subjected person to carry his pack up to one mile. Jesus advocates going beyond the limit and carrying it two miles in protest of such oppression.

In these examples, Jesus is creatively finding ways to empower an oppressed people to take the initiative and assert their dignity. Rather than cower in submission, Jesus is encouraging nonviolent protest through the only means available to them. This, of course, will not change anything, at least not right away, but it will empower the oppressed to act courageously. His teaching has definite social and political implications. Jesus is proposing "a worldly spirituality in which the people at the bottom of society or under the thumb of imperial power learn to recover their humanity."[40]

40. Ibid., 182.

The final example is not an example of nonviolent direct action, but reflects on life within an impoverished community, "Give to everyone who begs from you, and do not refuse anyone who wants to borrow from you" (5:42). Jesus encourages a radical egalitarian sharing within the community, supporting one another against such oppression.

These examples of creative nonviolent protest must not be severed from Jesus' instructions to love and pray for the enemy/oppressor. In other words, these actions that are aimed at empowering the oppressed are not to be performed vindictively, but out of genuine concern for the oppressor, realizing that the one who victimizes others is also a victim of his or her own victimization.

These examples are not laws; Jesus is not legislating specific behavior. He is offering an alternative to cowardly subjugation. Jesus is calling for creative, intentional, risky response to oppression that utilizes wit, humor, and some intelligent forethought.

According to Wink, Jesus' third way incorporates the following elements:

> Seize the moral initiative
> Find a creative alternative to violence
> Assert your own humanity and dignity as a person
> Meet force with ridicule and humor
> Break the cycle of humiliation
> Refuse to submit to or to accept the inferior position
> Expose the injustice of the system
> Take control of the power dynamic
> Shame the oppressor into repentance
> Stand your ground
> Make the Powers make decisions for which they are not prepared
> Recognize your own power
> Be willing to suffer rather than retaliate
> Force the oppressor to see you in a new light
> Deprive the oppressor of a situation where a show of force is effective
> Be willing to undergo the penalty of breaking unjust laws
> Die to fear of the old order and its rules
> Seek the oppressor's transformation[41]

Jesus' third way offers an alternative to passive withdraw and submission (flight), as well as armed, violent rebellion and retaliation

---

41. Ibid., 186–87.

(fight). His way enables the oppressed to stand against evil and expose evil, without being transformed by evil, thus pointing to a better way.

Dr. Martin Luther King Jr. so embodied Jesus' ethic of nonviolence that it became a social movement. His courageous confrontation of evil with the power of love became the liberating force behind the civil rights movement. He believed that nonviolent resistance was the most potent weapon an oppressed people could use in their quest for justice. But there were other, even more noble motivations that propelled Dr. King to the forefront as the primary inspiration for civil rights activists.

He understood that hate not only wrecks havoc on its victims, but it is equally as injurious and damaging to the one who hates. According to King, it is like an unchecked cancer that corrodes the personality and eats away at the soul. It not only blinds one to what is beautiful and ugly, it makes the one who indulges in it ugly. It scars the soul.

King also recognized that a strategy of resisting evil by refusing to cooperate with evil, standing one's ground in loving non-cooperation with evil, might possibly bring about a sense of shame in the opponent and break the cycle of violence. He understood that meeting hate with hate only intensifies it. He believed that love is the only force capable of transforming an enemy into a friend. He taught his followers that their aim was not to get rid of the enemy, but the enmity that empowered the enemy. Their aim was not to humiliate the offenders, but to win their friendship and understanding.

After a demonstration in 1962, King asked his most adamant supporters to make a commitment to: (1) meditate daily on the life and teachings of Jesus; (2) walk and talk in the manner of love, for God is love; (3) pray daily to be used by God so that all people might be free; and (4) refrain from all violence of fist, tongue and heart. King taught that all nonviolent resistance must be directed against evil itself, not the person who commits the evil.

How different from Rev King's voice has been the more recent surge of evangelical voices supporting violence. Dr. Charles Marsh, Professor of Religion at the University of Virginia, in his book, *Wayward Christian Soldiers: Freeing the Gospel from Political Captivity*, references the war sermons delivered by influential evangelical ministers during the period leading up to the Iraq war. He contended that the fall season of 2002 through the spring of 2003 will long be remembered as a sad chapter in the history of the Christian church. During those months many of

God's Dream for the World 75

the most respected voices in American evangelicalism blessed the president's war plans.

One leader claimed that our military forces in Iraq were preparing the way for the conversion of the Muslin world. Can you imagine? Another said, in his enthusiastic defense of the invasion of Iraq, that "in these urgent days we will seize the opportunity to advance the Kingdom of God." Still another not only endorsed the invasion, but extended the call for America "to exercise godly dominion and influence over every aspect and institution of human society." He boldly declared, "No power on earth can stop us."[42]

This is not the Spirit of Christ; this is not the Jesus of the Gospels. Whenever war is declared, even if it is in self-defense, it should be with anguish in our hearts. War means death and devastation. Military men and women will be killed, and what is called "collateral damage" involves intense and immense human suffering. The results of war are inevitable: families are decimated, children die, homes are destroyed, and poverty and disease follow in the wake of the devastation. Such is the nature of war. Such is the way of the principalities and powers of the world, not the kingdom of God.

Dr. Marsh was particularly appalled by a sermon from a highly popular evangelical preacher whose sermons are heard by millions of television viewers. In calling for support of the war he said, "God battles with people who oppose him, who fight against him and his followers." With a swat of the hand he dismissed the whole teaching and life of Jesus, saying that Jesus was speaking to individuals when he said to love our enemies. With one brief comment Jesus became totally irrelevant. Marsh comments on the sermon,

> The sermon's tone of supreme self-confidence is horrifying. There is no anguish, no dark night of struggle, no wrestling with Scripture . . . not a hint of apprehension, or words of caution, about the certain violence inflicted on civilians. There is no sense in which the believer must evaluate all moral decisions on the basis of the life and teachings of Jesus Christ.[43]

For these evangelicals, Jesus' capacity and authority to speak to believers struggling to counter the powers of terrorism were completely

---

42. Marsh, *Wayward Christian Soldiers*, 41–47.
43. Ibid., 44.

trivialized and dismissed. There were other evangelical voices that railed against the decision to go to war; Jim Wallis of Sojourners being one. But these voices were drowned out by the prominent evangelicals who received most of the media attention. How vastly different is the spirit and strategy of Jesus who declared, "Blessed are the peacemakers, for they will be called children of God" (Matt 5:9).

3

The Triumph of Love

For Christians, Jesus is the embodiment of divine love, and for most Christians the supreme demonstration of God's love revealed in Jesus is found in Jesus' self-giving unto death. The Apostle Paul expressed this in his letter to the Romans, "But God proves his love for us in that while we were still sinners Christ died for us" (Rom 5:8). The story of Jesus in the Gospels clearly indicates that there were powerful forces set against Jesus and the good news of God's reign that he proclaimed, taught, and manifested through his words and works of mercy. The religious leaders, inflamed with hostility, operated in conjunction and collaboration with the political authorities to seal Jesus' fate. Yet, from the very beginning of the Jesus movement, Jesus' followers believed that even though his death was the consequence of cruel hate and bitter animosity, God was at work in and through it, using it as a means of redemption. But in what sense is Jesus' death redemptive? How does Jesus' death have saving efficacy?

Theologians typically refer to this idea by the word "atonement." In common usage, the word is often employed to refer to the redemption or repair of a broken relationship, the process of making amends or restitution or putting things right. Etymologically, atonement means "at-one-ment," conveying the sense of reconciliation. In theological discourse, atonement theory generally involves arguments and explanations as to the means and ways Jesus' death brings salvation. My intention here is not to explore all the different shades and nuances of meaning conveyed through the various theories of atonement theology. I do, however, want to summarize as clearly as possible the popular traditional and evangelical teaching of substitutionary atonement, offer a short critique, and then present a more credible model, compatible with an inclusive gospel. This is important because most Christians are simply indoctrinated into substitutionary atonement theology and accept it as *the* Christian gospel.

SUBSTITUTIONARY ATONEMENT

What are the key components in substitutionary atonement theology? Dr. Robert P. Lightner, former theology professor at Dallas Theological Seminary, a school committed to traditional evangelical doctrine, wrote a book titled, *Evangelical Theology: A Survey and Review*, wherein he asserts that the substitutionary atonement of Christ is "an essential, indispensable truth in evangelicalism."[1] In his view, representative of many evangelicals, this is not an optional teaching or one open for debate.

Substitutionary atonement was one of the five principles (fundamentals) issued in 1895 at the Conference of Conservative Protestants (at Niagara Falls) that were claimed to be necessary for true Christian belief. The other four were the inerrancy of Scripture, the divinity of Jesus, the historicity of the virgin birth, and the physical, corporeal return of Jesus. According to religion expert, Phyllis Tickle, these five principles "along with the two others of the obligation to evangelize and belief in Jesus as personal Savior, have held firm as the core of evangelical Christianity."[2]

The following elements are generally always included in some way in the teaching of substitutionary atonement:

a. Jesus bore the penalty of sin (eternal death) resting on sinners, thus making possible the sinner's forgiveness.

b. Jesus paid the debt that sin incurs, making possible the sinner's acceptance before God and release from the obligation to God sin imposes.

c. Jesus purchased the sinner from the slave market of sin, setting the sinner free to now serve a new master.

d. Jesus bore the wrath or judgment of God against sin, thus propitiating God (satisfying God's offended sense of justice and holiness; satisfying God's honor).

---

1. Lightner, *Evangelical Theology*, 194–96.
2. Tickle, *The Great Emergence*, 66.

e. The sin of humanity was imputed to Christ on the cross while the righteousness of Jesus is imputed to the believer (credited to the believer's account) when the believer exercises saving faith. This is normally how traditional evangelicals understand the doctrine of justification. On the basis of this imputation the believer is declared "not guilty" and "righteous" before God—not practically, but positionally—that is, this is the believer's standing or position before God. The believer is clothed with the righteousness of Christ, therefore, all the believer's sins are covered—all of this being accomplished through the blood (the death) of Jesus who died for the sinner.

f. At the heart of all these basic concepts—penalty bearing, debt canceling, wrath placating, honor satisfying, holiness propitiating, etc.—is the idea that Jesus died in the sinner's place (in the sinner's stead or in the sinner's behalf), as a sinless, innocent sacrifice, taking on the sinner's punishment. The one who was sinless and did not deserve to die, became the willing sacrifice unto death on behalf of the sinner, so that it is possible for the sinner to be released, forgiven, justified, and accepted as righteous. Jesus' death solves the dilemma of how God can remain just and still justify (acquit, forgive, accept, reconcile) the sinner.

There are several major problems with this interpretation of Jesus' death. My following comments are framed around two critical aspects of this interpretation: first, how this view understands salvation and second, how this view imagines God.

One major problem with substitutionary atonement is that it reduces salvation to a legal transaction that has nothing to do with the actual transformation of the individual. When a person "believes" in this arrangement (accepts Christ as personal savior) the believer is forgiven all sin and justified (acquitted and declared righteous) before God. What is not explained (nor can it be adequately explained) in this manner of conceiving salvation is how this legal transaction actually effects change (salvation) in the inner life and outer conduct of the one who accepts the doctrine. Christ's death becomes the solution to the problem of the next world (heaven and hell), a fire insurance policy against divine retribution, but does nothing to effect moral transformation in this world.

In his excellent book, *The Divine Conspiracy*, Dallas Willard describes this as "bar-code faith."[3] Scanners are used in stores to read the bar-code on goods being purchased. It makes no difference to the scanner what is actually in the package, box, or bottle that contains the barcode. The electronic eye reads the code and a price is assigned. Many evangelical Christians believe that when the sinner makes a "decision" for Christ (invites Christ into his heart, trusts in Jesus' death for sin, confesses Christ publicly; various churches and traditions use different language) God "scans" the believer and then shifts the believer's sin onto Christ while Christ's righteousness is shifted to the believer's account in heaven, with the result that the believer's sin debt is paid in full and the believer is forgiven. This is usually explained as a private, personal act; a decision between the believer and God. When the believer makes this decision, God sees only the righteousness of Christ, regardless of what is actually in the heart and mind. In such a system the actual life and teachings of Jesus have little bearing on what it means to be a Christian.

The second major problem with substitutionary atonement is the way it pictures and imagines God. This interpretation of Jesus' death makes God the source of redemptive violence. According to this interpretation, God required/demanded a violent death for atonement to be made. God required the death of an innocent victim in order to satisfy God's offended sense of honor or pay off a penalty that God imposed. What kind of justice or God is this? Would a loving parent make forgiveness for the child conditioned upon a violent act?

Substitutionary atonement imagines a self-giving Son who gives his life in order to pay off/placate/satisfy/appease a harsh, vindictive Father. Even when God's union with Jesus is emphasized through Trinitarian configurations, the problem is not alleviated. No matter how positively nuanced the exposition, the result is still that God must save us from God.

Proponents of substitutionary atonement explain that God's holiness or justice demanded a substitute. Why? If God is sovereign, as advocates of substitutionary atonement contend, then God is the source of all justice. God is not subject to some sort of cosmic principle of justice outside of God's own nature. If God chooses to simply forgive sin the way a loving parent would forgive sin, without requiring some sort of pay off or sacrifice, there is no one to tell God that God is violating the demands of justice. God sets the standards of justice. In fact, substitu-

---

3. Willard, *The Divine Conspiracy*, 36.

tionary atonement reflects more of an ancient, primitive view of God than the view taught and embodied by Jesus of Nazareth. In the ancient world, sacrifice was demanded to placate the offended deity; to stay the deity's wrathful vengeance. Jesus imagined God as *Abba*—a loving, compassionate parent—seeking the best for God's children. The God of Jesus would have no need to save us from God's self.

The sacrificial language utilized in the New Testament is usually taken too literally by most Christians. For example, the reference to Christ's sacrificial death in Matthew 20:28 is often assumed to be a reference to substitutionary atonement. Nothing could be further from Jesus' mind, if indeed the saying originated with Jesus. In the passage Jesus rebukes his disciples for aspiring after positions of power and authority, calling them to a life of service, "Whoever wishes to be first among you must be your slave; just as the Son of Man came not to be served but to serve, and to give his life as a ransom for many" (Matt 20:27–28). New Testament scholar, M. Eugene Boring has pointed out that "ransom" (*lytron*) in the LXX (the Greek translation of the Old Testament) "had already lost its specific idea of release by paying off the captor and had come to mean simply 'rescue,' 'deliver' as an act of God's power (e.g., Exod 6:6; Deut 7:8)."[4]

To draw conclusions about substitutionary atonement from this imagery is to over-use the image and read into it what is not present. In the context, the liberation, deliverance, or redemption that Jesus is speaking of is a liberation from the need to pursue power, position, and prestige by being a faithful servant to all people, regardless of station, class, or rank. In this Gospel passage it is not Jesus' death alone that is the means of rescue or redemption; rather, it is Jesus' life as a whole, offered up selflessly and sacrificially in service for the good of others, even unto death. Matthew changes Mark's simple conjunction "and" to "just as" in order to clarify that Jesus as Son of Man is the model for the disciples own lives and ministry. They are "rescued" from a life of self-aggrandizement and egotism by following Jesus in a life of humble service to others. Substitutionary atonement is clearly not in the picture.

The sacrificial images employed in the New Testament, particularly by Paul in his letters, are metaphors of salvation and should not be taken literally. For example, when Paul says that Christ's death brings redemption Paul is not suggesting that Jesus' death was the literal price paid to

---

4. Boring, *The Gospel of Matthew*, 399.

God (or to Satan as some have argued) to secure the disciples' release from the penalty or power of sin. Rather, Paul is simply saying that Christ's death is the means of deliverance/redemption, but he does not explain or elaborate how it works. This is why theologians and biblical interpreters talk about "theories" of atonement; the biblical writers use images and metaphors that are left loose and hanging, and are therefore subject to various interpretations.

It could well be that when Paul references the death of Christ he intends to gather up the full significance and meaning of the Christ Event. It is quite possible that the first Christians spoke of Jesus' death as a way of summing up the redemptive meaning of the whole story of Jesus. For example, consider Romans 5:6–11,

> For while we were still weak, at the right time Christ died for the ungodly. Indeed, rarely will anyone die for a righteous person—though perhaps for a good person someone might actually dare to die. But God proves his love for us in that while we still were sinners Christ died for us. Much more, surely then, now that we have been justified by his blood, will we be saved through him from the wrath of God. For if while we were enemies, we were reconciled to God through the death of his Son, much more surely, having been reconciled, will we be saved by his life. But much more than that, we even boast in God through our Lord Jesus Christ, through whom we have now received reconciliation.

Several references in the above passage are made to Jesus' death: "Christ died for the ungodly"; "while we still were sinners Christ died for us"; "we have been justified by his blood"; "were reconciled to God through the death of his Son." Christ bore the sin—the hate and animosity of the world—all the way to the cross, and by bearing it he exhausted it, he overcame it, providing a way for sinners ("the weak," "the ungodly," the "enemies") to be made right with God and one another, to be reconciled to God and all people. But then Paul says that having been reconciled through his death, we will "be saved by his life," and in his closing statement he mentions neither Jesus' death nor life, but simply says that through our Lord Jesus Christ "we have now received reconciliation."

It is likely that Paul, following the practice of disciples of Jesus before him, employed the language of sacrificial death to gather up the meaning and impact of the whole story of Jesus, the Christ—his life, death, and resurrection—in its entirety. The resurrection served as God's vindication, God's "yes" to Jesus' sacrificial life and death.

Unfortunately, the sacrificial images employed by Paul and other New Testament writers carry a lot of baggage. When we think of sacrifice in a religious context it is natural to think of a worshiper offering a sacrifice in order to satisfy the honor or turn back the wrath of an offended or angry god. The God of Jesus, however, does not need to be propitiated. God's attitude toward God's children is love. Love does not need or require a sacrificial victim. Jesus did not have to die in order to satisfy some need in God or to pay off some debt owed to God. God is able to forgive freely. Humans crucified Jesus. Jesus was not born to die as if his main purpose on earth was to die on the cross. Jesus didn't have to die in order to make atonement to God for sin. We are the ones needing atonement, we are the ones needing to change, not God.

When the Roman emperor, Constantine, declared the Roman Empire Christian, Paul's sacrificial metaphors became the prevailing way of talking about Christ's death and the Christian's salvation. Jesus' proclamation and teaching about God's new world and his radical call to deliberate nonviolence and love for enemies was ignored and fell out of favor. Jesus' countercultural teaching, his critique of conventional wisdom, and his confrontation of the powers that be became subversive to the church's role in the state religion. Salvation was reduced to an individual transaction or relationship between the believer and God. Paul took preference over Jesus because Paul's sacrificial metaphors could more easily be adapted to the interests of the empire. The *Abba* of Jesus, the loving, caring, merciful Father/Mother was replaced as the dominant image of God with a God of wrath who demanded the violent death of a sinless substitute as a ransom for sinners.

The nonviolent God of Jesus, however, is incompatible with a God who makes a horrendous act of violence a divinely required act of atonement. A more credible version of the gospel sees Jesus' death, not as a payment for sin demanded by God, but as the culmination of his nonviolent, self-giving love poured out for others, even unto death (Phil 2:5–8).

So how might we understand the sacrificial language in the New Testament? To say that Jesus died "for" us, "in our behalf," or "in our place" does not mean Jesus had to assume our judgment, sin debt, or punishment. It may simply mean that in representing us as the "Son of Man," the archetypal human being, he bore the wrath, hate, and animosity of the world. Not, of course, in any literal sense. In a literal sense he bore the wrath of *some* of the religious leaders, the judgment of Pilate who acted on behalf of Rome, the humiliation and condemnation of the Roman soldiers assigned to him, and the insults, mockery, and anger of the mob who took sport in his crucifixion, but he did not literally bear all the sins of the world or the punishment of God. In a symbolic, representative way he bore the suffering, hate, and evil of the world.

JESUS' NONVIOLENT ATONEMENT

Biblical scholar, Raymond Schwager has observed that in the Old Testament there are six hundred passages of explicit violence and over one thousand verses where God's own violent actions of punishment are described. There are over a hundred passages where God expressly commands others to kill people.[5] When confronted with the violence in the Bible, most Christians simply duck the issue.

Of course that's just half the story. There are a number of expressions of God's tender mercy and love in the Hebrew Bible as well. God is often depicted as patient, gracious, and forgiving in God's relationship with Israel and the world. I have a real affinity for the book of Jonah because it depicts God's compassion and love for a wicked, violent people who were not in a covenant relationship with God. God still cared for them and sought their redemption.

When we embrace the violence we read about in the Bible, we perpetuate and sanctify the worst of the human condition. Walter Wink explains that "the violence of the Bible is the necessary precondition for the gradual perception of the meaning of violence."[6] We have a tendency to project our fears, shame, and anger onto God. We also project these attitudes and feelings onto one another as a way of trying to justify and get rid of them. This process is called scapegoating, because it is the process of transferring our guilt and sin onto someone else. Unfortunately, it is a common human pattern.

Projecting our shame, guilt, and sin onto others as a way of dealing with these dark forces does offers a kind of temporary relief. We convince ourselves that the other is the enemy and the other deserves our hate; this enables us to hate without feeling guilty. It doesn't seem to matter how educated we are either, we still do it—the educated, however,

---

5. Referenced by Wink, *The Powers That Be*, 84.
6. Ibid., 85–86.

do it with more sophistication and subtlety. When Hitler came to power in Germany and made scapegoating official policy, Germany was the most educated nation in the world.

There is no end to the cycle once a culture is committed to it. Chauvenists hate women; radical feminists hate men. Liberals hate conservatives; conservatives hate liberals. The wealthy despise the poor and the poor despise the rich. There is no end to the divisions and the hostility.

Religion becomes evil when we use religion to disguise hate and prejudice. When we hate and despise others under the banner of God and theological correctness, religion becomes deadly. Christianity has been just as guilty of this as any other religious tradition. Many Christians who have worshiped Jesus as their personal Savior have moved on to make scapegoats of others, dividing the world between "us" and "them." Richard Rohr has noted how many Christians "with utter irony, worshipped Jesus as the Scapegoat on Sundays and made scapegoats of Jews, Moslems, and other Christian denominations, heretics, sinners, pagans, the poor and almost anybody who was not like them the other six days of the week."[7]

Jesus, of course, refused to do this. Instead of dividing the world between the righteous and unrighteous, Jesus welcomed all people as his brothers and sisters. An American soldier was killed in France in World War II. His friends wanted to bury him in the local Catholic cemetery. They went to the priest who refused their request because their friend was Protestant. But he allowed them to bury him in an open space just outside the fence that enclosed the cemetery. Before the Americans could get the grave dug, darkness fell, so they decided to stop for the night and finish the next morning. When they returned the next day to complete the dig they couldn't find the grave. They went back to the priest who laughed and then explained, "Well, last night I couldn't sleep. I kept thinking about what I told you. So I went out and moved the fence. You can bury your friend in our cemetery."

This is what Jesus does—he moves the fence so that no one is excluded. Actually, he does more than move the fence; he demolishes all the barriers that divide us.

In John's Gospel Jesus is identified as "the Lamb of God who takes away the sin of the world" (John 1:29). He takes it away by absorbing it

7. Rohr, *Hope Against Darkness*, 150.

in himself. In bearing it he exposes it and ends the cycle of scapegoating, the cycle of denial and projection, the cycle of hate and violence. Though Jesus dies a violent death, he doesn't take away our sin through violence. In God's kingdom there is no redemptive violence, only redemptive suffering.

The mention of Jesus as the Lamb of God would recall to those familiar with Israel's story, the Passover lamb. In the story of Israel's exodus from Egypt, the blood of the Passover lamb marked the houses of the people of Israel, pointing to their deliverance from bondage and the beginning of a new way of life in a covenant relationship with God. The killing of animals as religious ritual seems crude to us today, as it should, but of course, animal sacrifice was common to ancient religion. The point of connection between Jesus and the Passover lamb is what Jesus' death points toward. As the blood of the Passover lamb symbolized God's deliverance of Israel from bondage and the beginning of a new way of life, so the death of Jesus points the way toward a new kind of liberation—deliverance from bondage to hate and condemnation. Jesus died as a scapegoat to put an end to all scapegoating. He bore the violence of the powers that be in order to put an end to all violence.

In identifying Jesus as the Lamb of God there may also be an allusion to the suffering servant song in Isaiah. Like a lamb led to be slaughtered, Jesus did not retaliate, seek revenge, or wish curses upon his enemies. He went to the cross—a cruel means of execution devised by the Romans not only to kill but to humiliate those so sentenced—without wishing harm upon the religious leaders, Pilate, the Roman soldiers, or the hostile crowd. The cross is sacred because here is where Jesus exposed the evil of scapegoating, the evil of transferring hate and projecting fear onto others. It is where Jesus chose the higher way, the way of forgiveness and peace over the way of revenge and retribution. Jesus absorbed the hate and refused to pass it on. Richard Rohr has expressed this reality beautifully,

> Christians indeed have a strange image of God: a naked, bleeding man dying on a cross. Now let's be honest. If you were going to create a religion, would any of you ever have thought up this image of God? I mean, if I had been setting out to manufacture a religion, I would have manufactured "seven habits for highly effective people." I would have a big sun or a big golden orb for the symbol of God and I would have called God "the Force." But

never in a thousand years would I have thought of an image of God as a naked, bleeding, poor man, rejected by society and religion.... He does not use his suffering and death as power *over* others to punish them, but as power *for* others to transform them.... In one sense or another, all ancient religions felt we had to spill our blood to get to God. God was distant, demanding and dangerous. God couldn't possibly love me in my radical unworthiness. What we have in the mystery of the crucified Jesus is the turning around of all primal religion. No more human sacrifice, no more animal sacrifice, no more Jansenism (beating yourself so you can be worthy of this God who basically doesn't like you). Instead of our spilling blood to get to God we have God spilling blood to get to us![8]

Paul (or a Christian leader in the Pauline tradition) explained in the letter to the Colossians that Jesus' death on the cross "disarmed the rulers and authorities and made a public example of them, triumphing over them in it" (Col 2:15). Christ exposed the evil of the principalities and powers, not in order to banish them forever, but in order to redeem them.

John's Gospel speaks of the prince of the world being judged on the cross (John 12:31). The "prince of the world" is the mythical archetype of evil, the representative of the powers of darkness. The powers of evil are judged in that they are exposed and seen for what that really are. Their true nature is revealed in the crucifixion scene. The judgment is rendered, however, not in order to condemn them, but to save them (John 3:17). Judas is a good example of Jesus' intention. Jesus never closed the door on Judas. He could always come back. There is no point of no return. Only a nonviolent, non-vengeful, non-retaliatory response can unmask and expose the powers of evil for what they are, making conversion possible.

Gospel truth can be found in the oddest places. I came home one evening and Jordan, my son who was a senior in high school at the time, was watching the movie, *The Bad News Bears*. It played all week on one of the cable stations. For some reason I was drawn in and watched the rest of the movie with my son.

In the championship game, the coach of the opposing team loses his composure with his son who is pitching. He calls time, walks sternly out to the mound, screams at his son, and pushes him down. He hu-

8. Ibid., 151.

miliates his son in front of everyone, appearing ridiculous and foolish. As Coach Buttermaker (Billy Bob Thornton) watches this scene unfold something clicks—he sees himself and he doesn't like what he sees—and he changes. He experiences in that moment of recognition a kind of repentance and becomes a better human being.

This is what can happen when we bear the hate and animosity of the other—it may cause the offender to pause long enough to see himself—and decide to change. Then again, it may not. The offender may be too blinded by his greed, hate, or prejudice. Whatever the outcome or consequences, this is the way of the cross of Christ.

Jesus was a revolutionary, but not the kind we normally think of. Most revolutions simply replace the people in power and employ basically the same methods of power to enforce their will, which is about like rearranging the chairs on the Titanic. Jesus built a new boat. The power of the cross is the power to transform human relationships through forgiveness.

FORGIVENESS AND THE TRANSFORMING POWER OF LOVE

During the Los Angeles riots in the aftermath of the Rodney King verdict, Reginald Denny was dragged from his truck and mercilessly beaten. After his painful recovery, he met face-to-face with his attackers, shook hands with them, and forgave them. A reporter, commenting on the scene, wrote, "It is said that Mr. Denny is suffering from brain damage." So often forgiveness seems to be in short supply in our society, even in the Christian community, and yet it stands at the center of the Christian gospel.

The words that Jesus spoke during his last meal with the disciples, when they celebrated the Passover together, most likely reflect Jesus' own perspective regarding his death. In Mark's Gospel when Jesus passed the cup to his disciples he said, "This is my blood of the covenant, which is poured out for many" (Mark 14:24). It is probable that Jesus interpreted his death as the seal of God's covenant with God's people, the people of the new creation. The death of Jesus was considered by his followers to be the bond that sealed the eschatological renewal of God's covenant.

Matthew's Gospel basically follows the Markan text, but adds the idea of forgiveness of sins. In Matthew, Jesus says, "Drink from it, all of you, for this is my blood of the covenant, which is poured out for the forgiveness of sins" (Matt 26:28). Matthew's intention here was not to make a causal connection between Jesus' death and forgiveness; that is, Matthew was not saying that Jesus' death was necessary in order to procure the forgiveness of sins. Earlier in Matthew's narrative, the author makes clear that Jesus, as Son of Man, is given authority to forgive sins—an authority that is given to all human beings (Matt 9:2–8). No sacrifice is necessary. All human beings are given the authority and capacity to forgive. Matthew's version of Jesus' instructions regarding the cup stresses the point that forgiveness of sins is basic and central to the renewed covenant between God and God's people sealed through Jesus' death.

Luke's Gospel emphasizes forgiveness in the way the writer narrates the passion story. When Judas led the group to Jesus to arrest him, Luke says that the disciples asked, "Lord, should we strike with the sword?" Then, according to Luke, one of the disciples struck the servant of the high priest cutting off his ear. In response Jesus said, "No more of this!" And he touched his ear and healed him" (Luke 22:49–51). Luke writes,

> Then Jesus said to the chief priests, the officers of the temple police, and the elders who had come for him, "Have you come out with swords and clubs as if I were a bandit? When I was with you day after day in the temple, you did not lay hands on me. But this is your hour, and the power of darkness!" Luke 22:52–53

Jesus had exercised authority over the powers of darkness, healing the demonized (Luke 4:36). He gave that same power to the twelve (9:1) and then to the seventy (10:17–20). Now he surrenders to the powers of darkness. It is their time to prevail. Herein lies the paradox, irony, and ingenuity of the cross. In Paul's correspondence with the church at Corinth, Paul says that the cross of Christ, which was regarded as foolishness among the Greeks and was a scandalous offense to Jews, was nevertheless, the very wisdom and power of God (1 Cor 1:18–25). Jesus' self-surrender unto death became the basis for the defeat of the powers of darkness.

The only way to overcome the darkness is by walking through the darkness. The power of God's new world is not the power to beat back the darkness by means of violence and force; it is, rather, the power to dispel and redeem the darkness through love and forgiveness. The power of God's reign is the power to heal and make whole by bearing the violence in one's own self, thereby exposing and exhausting it.

Luke makes a special effort to emphasize Jesus' innocence; that he did nothing to merit this response from the religious and political powers that be. Three times Luke has Pilate declare Jesus' innocence (23:4–5, 13–15, 22). In the final scene of the crucifixion the Roman centurion says, "Certainly this man was innocent [or righteous/just]" (23:47). By contrast, in Mark (followed by Matthew) the centurion says, "Truly this man was God's Son" (15:39). Luke tells the story his way in order to emphasize that Jesus did nothing to deserve the judgment rendered by Pilate and the harsh, torturous treatment inflicted upon him by the Roman soldiers. He was handed over unjustly to be crucified. Yet Jesus did not respond to hate with hate, but rather, with love.

Unique to Luke are three scenes that highlight Jesus' nonviolent, forgiving response. First, Jesus laments the tragic suffering and violence that will befall Jerusalem where many innocent women and children will suffer. In his unjust suffering, Jesus is joined to the plight of all the innocent ones who suffer the ravages of violence (23:27–31).

Second, Jesus pronounces forgiveness upon his enemies from the cross, "Father, forgive them; for they do not know what they are doing" (23:34). In the NRSV this statement is in brackets noting that "other ancient authorities lack the sentence." The external manuscript evidence for its inclusion or exclusion is fairly evenly divided, but it is generally pointed out by textual scholars arguing for its authenticity that a scribe would most likely delete the statement, rather than add it. Tensions between Christians and Jews in the early church could have led to its omission, and it is quite possible that a scribe may have found the prayer to be morally unjustifiable. After all, Christians have through the centuries largely ignored it.

Third, Jesus forgives one of the criminals crucified next to him. Luke intentionally alters Mark's account where both criminals ridicule Jesus (Mark 15:32). In Luke, one of the criminals is confessional and repentant. Luke's scene gives us the gospel in miniature: Jesus dying a cruel, unjust death and yet bearing it in grace, extending mercy and forgiveness. Luke writes,

> One of the criminals who were hanged there kept deriding him and saying, "Are you not the Messiah? Save yourself and us!" But the other rebuked him, saying, "Do you not fear God, since you are under the same sentence of condemnation? And we indeed have been condemned justly, for we are getting what we

The Triumph of Love 91

deserve for our deeds, but this man has done nothing wrong." Then he said, "Jesus, remember me when you come into your kingdom." He replied, "Truly I tell you, today you will be with me in Paradise." Luke 23:39–43.

The cry, "remember me" is a common expression found in the Hebrew Bible employed as an appeal for grace (see 1 Sam 1:11). The response of the two criminals in some ways parallels the response of the tax collector and the Pharisee (Luke 18:9–14).

Luke narrates the story of an innocent, blameless victim bearing the hate, hostility, and unjust suffering inflicted upon him by the powers that be. Jesus absorbs the injustice and refuses to lash out or even harbor anger in his heart. He acts with compassion, mercy, and grace. He identifies with the innocent who suffer due to the actions of others. He forgives his tormentors and executioners. He acts in grace, bestowing hope upon one who calls out for mercy.

The second scene mentioned above is the one that has given Christians the most trouble, and the one that has been the most neglected in Christendom—"Father, forgive them; for they do not know what they are doing" (Luke 23:33). The Jewish religious leaders plotted it, the Roman authorities executed it, and the Roman soldiers and angry mob took sadistic pleasure in it. How could they not know what they were doing?

United Methodist Bishop, Will Willimon, in a conversation with a group of seminary faculty, remarked what a bad book had been written by a professor at another seminary. He commented that he expected a bad book from someone who was such a jerk. After the group dissolved, one colleague lingered behind. He said to Willimon, "The person whom you just trashed was the only person to stick by me in my divorce, the only person personally to offer me help and comfort. But I want you to know that I intend to forgive you for your boorish insensitivity. You are forgiven." Willimon commented, "Until I got the forgiveness for being an insensitive boor, I did not know I was an insensitive boor."[9]

The Jewish religious leaders were ridding Israel of a heretic. The Roman imperial authorities were keeping law and order. The violence-loving mob figured that the rebel was getting what he deserved. They didn't know what they were doing—crucifying God's Messiah.

---

9. Willimon, *Thank God It's Friday*, 11–12.

We would expect some acknowledgement of wrongdoing. We would require heart-felt remorse. We would demand sorrowful contrition and gut-wrenching repentance. But from the cross Jesus extended preemptive forgiveness. The enormity of the cruelty is met only by the magnitude of grace. Before confession, repentance, or any acknowledgement of wrongdoing—"Father, forgive them."

Sometimes we forgive in order to get away from the wrongdoer. Like the woman who told Willimon, "My ex-husband has done everything he can to make my life miserable—before and after the divorce. I am so eaten up with anger and resentment that the doctor says it has affected my health. Can't sleep. Can't eat. I've tried everything. Now, there's nothing left for me to do but to forgive and forget him and hope to God I'll be done with him forever and he'll forever be done with me."[10] Sometimes that is the best we can do, given the tragedy of the human condition and the hurt we cause one another.

We forgive in order to breathe again and get on with life. But Jesus doesn't forgive in order to drive us away and forget about us. Jesus forgives in order to draw us close. Without such amazing grace there would be no hope or real possibility for reconciliation and new beginnings. Threats of punishment may alter behavior but cannot transform the heart. On the cross Jesus responded to his enemies with a preemptive strike of forgiveness. Who would have thought?

Love has transforming power. A family is out for a drive on a Sunday afternoon. It is a pleasant afternoon, and they relax at a leisurely pace down the road. Suddenly, the two children begin to beat their father on the back, "Daddy, Daddy, stop the car! There's a kitten back there on the road!" The father says, "So, we're having a drive."

"But daddy, you must stop and pick it up."

"I don't have to stop and pick it up."

"But if you don't, it will die."

"We don't have room for any more animals. We have a zoo already. No more animals."

"But Daddy, are you going to just let it die?"

"Be quiet, children, we are going to have a pleasant drive."

"But Daddy, we never thought you would be so mean and cruel as to let a kitten die."

---

10. Ibid., 12.

The Triumph of Love   93

Then, the final word. Mother turns to her husband and says, "Dear, you'll have to stop." So he turns the car around and pulls off the road. "You kids stay here in the car. I'll see about it."

He goes out to pick up the little kitten; it is skin and bones, sore-eyed, and full of fleas. When he reaches down to pick it up, with its last bit of energy the kitten bristles, baring tooth and claw. It scratches him. He picks up the kitten by the loose skin at the neck, brings it over to the car, and says, "Don't touch it. It's probably got leprosy."

Back home they go. The children give the kitten several baths, about a gallon of warm milk, and plead with Dad, "Can we let it stay in the house just tonight? Tomorrow we'll fix it a place in the garage." By this time the father is whipped, "Sure, take my bedroom; the whole house is already a zoo."

They fix it a comfortable bed. Several weeks pass. Then one day the father walks in, feels something rub against his leg, looks down, and there is a cat. He reaches down toward the cat, carefully checking to see that no one is watching. When the cat sees his hand, it does not bare its claws and hiss; instead it arches its back to receive a caress.

Is that the same cat? It's not the same frightened, hurt, hissing kitten on the side of the road. And we know what made the difference.[11]

In Luke's Gospel repentance is often connected to the gift of forgiveness. Luke summarizes the message of John the Baptist as a "baptism of repentance for the forgiveness of sins" (Luke 3:3). At the end of his Gospel, Luke summarizes the message given to the disciples by the risen Christ, "repentance and forgiveness of sins is to be proclaimed in his name to all nations, beginning from Jerusalem" (24:47). Forgiveness can be extended to others without repentance, just as Jesus forgave his killers; but forgiveness cannot be experienced without a change of mind and heart. The enjoyment and experience of the gift of forgiveness always involves some element of letting go in both the giver and the receiver.

Christian writer, educator, and former pastor, Calvin Miller shared a wonderful story about his son who liked to "save" things until they could no longer be saved. Miller said that one afternoon when they were having a family picnic near a stream, his son took a milk carton and scooped up three tadpoles. He called them Peter, Paul, and Mary. He took them home and kept them in a jar until the water turned green. Calvin would ask him, "Tim, what are you doing with those tadpoles?"

11. Craddock, *Craddock Stories*, 24–25.

His son would respond, "Dad, I'm saving them." First Peter died, then Paul. Mary was the lone survivor and actually achieved froghood. She grew legs and lost her tail, but she wasn't happy. Calvin said to his son, "Tim, if you save Mary much longer, she's going to end up like Peter and Paul. You've got to let her go." He agreed. So they drove back to her ancestral home, walked down to the stream, opened up the jar, and as she hopped out they sang a few bars of "Born Free."[12]

The hope of the world, as well as our own spiritual, emotional, and physical health, depends on our capacity to let go of our pride and stubbornness, our need to be right, and our need to control people, circumstances and outcomes. Perhaps the most difficult thing we must let go of is our anger.

In one sense anger is simply a natural response to feeling threatened. Sometimes it may even serve a useful or necessary purpose in an emergency situation. There are very few instances, however, where the long term use of anger will be helpful, and no instance I can think of where it is necessary. Harboring anger leads to bitterness and resentment. When we harbor anger and refuse to forgive we create grievance stories. Our grievance stories describe the painful things we have endured but not healed from. These are the kind of stories that when we tell them make us angry or hurt all over again. Our spiritual, emotional, and even physical well-being is negatively impacted when we relive these stories.

Fr Richard Rohr shares a personal story that dramatically illustrates the impact and power of grievance stories and forgiveness. His mother, whom he describes as "an earthy, farming woman, no sentimentalist," was dying. He was sitting beside her bed, telling her that he was going to miss her when she said suddenly, "I want to hear it from him." He said, "What?" She said, "Him." He said, "You mean Daddy?" His father was eighty-four but the kids still called him Daddy. She said, "Yea, I want to hear if he's going to miss me." For weeks, says Rohr, Daddy had been telling her he loved her and was going to miss her.

He came over and told her again. She said, "I don't believe it." Fr Rohr responded, "Mother, you're a few hours from death. You can't say that." She persisted, "I don't believe it." Her husband then asked her to forgive him for anything he ever did to hurt her. She was silent. Fr Rohr had to play the role of priest. He said, "Mother, you're soon going to be before God. You don't want to come before God without forgiving ev-

---

12. Miller, *Into the Depths of God*, 24–25.

erybody." She replied, "I forgive everybody." He said, "But do you forgive Daddy?" She was silent again. His father jumped in, "Honey, I never fooled around with any other women." She exclaimed, "Well, I know that, I know that." They all knew that. But what they didn't know, was what it was that she couldn't forgive.

Fr Rohr urged, "Mother, you know the Our Father. You're only going to get as much forgiveness from God as you've given. Now, you've got to forgive Daddy." She kept her eyes closed. Fr Rohr pulled out every priestly and pastoral trick he knew. Nothing was getting through. Then he said, "Mother, I'm going to put one hand on your heart and I'm going to pray that it gets real soft." As he prayed, he started kissing the other hand. She sighed, "That melts me. When you kiss my hand like that, now I've got to do it." After a pause she said, "I'm a stubborn woman, all my life I've been a stubborn woman." Fr Rohr said, "Well, mother we all knew that. Now, look at Daddy and tell him." She looked over at him and said, "Rich, I forgive you." Fr Rohr prompted her, "Now mother, the other half—ask Daddy's forgiveness." She struggled with this, but she summoned her energy and said, "Rich, I ask your forgiveness."

Then she said, "That's it, that's it. That's what I had to do." She had been talking for days about "a mesh." She would say, "There's a mesh I'm trying to get through." No one knew what she was talking about. Fr Rohr asked her, "Mother, do you think that was the mesh?" She said, "It's gone. The mesh is gone." Next she declared, "God, I pray that I mean this forgiveness from my heart." That was only four days before she died. Then she said to her son, "Tell the girls (referring to his two sisters and his sister-in-law) to do this early and not to wait 'til now. They'll understand a woman's heart and the way a man can hurt a woman."

Fr Rohr speculates that after fifty-four years of marriage, maybe there were little grudges or maybe some big ones, they didn't know. Maybe it had something to do with space. She was the flower woman and her husband was the grass man and they were always fighting for more space. Sometimes he would run over her flowers with the lawn mower. Maybe that was a symbol of something much deeper in their souls. Who knows; they didn't know. But whatever it was, she finally let it go. Fr Rohr said to his mother, "Mother, aren't you glad you said it." She exclaimed, "I'm so happy, I'm so happy."[13]

---

13. Rohr, *Hope Against Darkness*, 141–43.

Life is too short to hang on to all the grudges, resentments, and grievances we retell again and again.

It's important not to be confused about what forgiveness is and what it is not. Forgiveness is not denying, minimizing, or condoning the hurt or the severity of the offense caused by another. If something terrible was done to us, forgiveness is not saying, "That wasn't so bad."

Forgiveness is not forgetting. We may ask God to help us forget, but forgiveness is not forgetting. In fact, it is helpful to celebrate our capacity to forgive and to remember our hurts from the point of view of healing, not from that of helpless victimization. By remembering, we are able to offer compassion and support to others who are struggling with forgiveness.

Forgiveness, also, is not the elimination of all consequences. Some wrongs require restitution. For example, if a person under the influence of drugs or alcohol causes physical harm to another, forgiveness does not eliminate the need for restitution, for compensation and restorative justice. It's not enough to say, "I'm sorry." Restitution is required. Forgiveness does not mean that there are no consequences.

The only thing that can possibly break the cycle of hate, violence, and retaliation in our world is forgiveness. There can be no reconstruction, no reconciliation, no coming together and healing of persons and nations without forgiveness. But forgiveness is a hard sell. It defies all reason, logic, and worldly standards of worthiness. But without forgiveness there can be no future. We have hurt each other in too many ways.

Denzel Washington stars in the movie, *The Hurricane*, which is the story of professional boxer Rubin "Hurricane" Carter. At the height of his boxing career in the 1960's, he was falsely accused of murder by a racist police force and sentenced to prison for the remainder of his natural life.

While Carter is in prison, Lesra, a young black boy who has read Carter's autobiography befriends him. As the friendship deepens, the boy introduces Carter to some of his adult friends who become convinced of Carter's innocence and commit to helping him as his amateur lawyers and detectives. After twenty years in prison he is granted a new trial. As they await the verdict, Carter and Lesra share their thoughts. Carter says, "We've come a long way, huh, little brother? Lesra nods and says, "Rubin, I just want you to know that if this doesn't work, I'm bustin' you outta here." "You are?" says Carter. Lesra retorts, "Yeah, that's right, I'm bustin' you outta here."

After a moment of silence Carter suggests that they were not brought together by chance. He then says, "Hate put me in prison. Love's gonna bust me out." Lesra responds, "Just in case love doesn't, I'm gonna bust you outta here." Carter laughs. He reaches out to touch Lesra's face and wipe away a tear. Clenching his hand he says, "You already have, Lesra."[14]

Love can set loose the chains of hate and bitterness that bind and enslave us. Love is able to liberate us from a sense of hopelessness and despair, and from the need to retaliate and seek revenge.

Christian writer and teacher, Bruce Larson told about an experience he had years ago when his kids were small. They bought a baby parakeet—a poor, bald thing with no feathers, which they named Jeremiah. Jeremiah grew into a very talented bird. He could say, "Give me a kiss, baby" and "I'm a Presbyterian." The bird had the run of the house. One day he walked outside only to discover that Jeremiah was on his shoulder. As he turned to go back inside, Jeremiah flew off never to be seen again. He had been a member of the family for eight years. He thought his kids would blame him, but they never once said, "How could you?" Instead, noted Larson, "they loved me, and felt sorry for me." Larson added, "those are rare moments—when we are forgiven much."[15] The gospel of Jesus is a rare gospel, but it is the hope of the world.

Albert Einstein said that the world's problems cannot be solved at the same level of thinking that caused them. Forgiveness reflects a new level of thinking. It enables us to let go of all our grievances, to transcend all our differences, and to see the other as our sister and brother in the family of God.

THE COSMIC CHRIST, JUDGMENT, AND THE VICTORY OF GOD

It is not exactly clear what the first followers of Jesus meant when they identified him as "Messiah," "Son of God," and "Son of Man." It is even more unclear what Jesus himself may have believed, if he in any way claimed, identified himself, or understood his mission in light of these titles. What is clear, however, is that Jesus spoke and acted with an un-

---

14. *The Hurricane*, Universal Pictures, 1999.
15. Larson, *Luke*, 140–41.

precedented authority among his peers. For example, Mark observes that when Jesus taught in the synagogue at Capernaum, "They were astounded at his teaching, for he taught them as one having authority, and not as the scribes" (1:22). Then, after Jesus rebukes and casts out an unclean spirit, Mark says, "They were all amazed, and they kept on asking one another, "What is this? A new teaching—with authority! He commands even the unclean spirits, and they obey him" (1:27).

Whatever the specific meaning of the titles of Jesus in a pre-Easter and post-Easter context, without question, the historic Jesus of Nazareth was convinced that he would have a central role in the establishment of God's new world and that God's future reign was dawning and impinging upon the present evil world through his words and works, particularly his healings of the diseased, the disabled, and the demonized (Matt 12:22–29). The Gospels proclaim that Jesus of Nazareth was an authority on life in God's new world. And when Jesus called disciples to follow him and learn from him how to live in God's new world, he automatically asserted a moral and spiritual authority over their lives.

While Jesus never required or even invited worship, he did expect his followers to emulate his spiritual practices, obey his teachings, and join him in announcing and serving God's cause (kingdom) in the world. Therefore, Jesus' role and function as judge began when he claimed the authority to be a moral force in the lives of his disciples. Following his vindication/resurrection, his followers began to proclaim him as Lord and judge of the world. For example, in the book of Acts, Paul proclaims in his address to the intellectuals in Athens that Jesus is the man through whom God will judge the world in righteousness/justice (Acts 17:31).

What does it mean for Jesus to be acknowledged as judge of humanity? Dualistic versions of Christianity commonly view Christ's role as one of determining a person's eternal destiny. But as we have argued in chapter 2, Jesus' passion for the kingdom of God related to this life and this world, not an afterlife in some other world.

It's important for Bible readers to realize that all the judgment texts found in the New Testament have been influenced to some degree by apocalyptic ideas and symbols. It is significant, too, that the grounds for judgment in these texts all relate to the kind of life lived, not one's particular beliefs.

Paul, in his letter to the Romans, says that on the day of God's "righteous judgment,"

> He will repay according to each one's deeds: to those who by patiently doing good seek for glory and honor and immortality, he will give eternal life; while for those who are self-seeking and who obey not the truth but wickedness, there will be wrath and fury. There will be anguish and distress for everyone who does evil, the Jew first and also the Greek, but glory and honor and peace for everyone who does good, the Jew first and also the Greek. For God shows no partiality. Rom 2:6–11

This is typical of the judgment texts in the New Testament. These texts reflect apocalyptic images and make the life one has lived the basic criterion for judgment. Dualistic versions of Christianity have tended to literalize the apocalyptic language in these texts. Proponents of an inclusive gospel reject the literalization of the apocalyptic elements in these Scriptures, but still take seriously Jesus' role as judge, as well as the meaning and implications of judgment.

Dr. Fred Craddock told about being at a conference where he was one of the speakers. It was a rural setting and between sessions he got in his car and drove around to clear his head and get ready for his next presentation. He found an old cemetery and decided to look around. While reading the markers, he found a plot with a huge stone. Etched in the stone was the family name, with burial plots stretching out on both sides for some distance. Instead of dirt covering the graves, they had concrete slabs extending their full length and size.

Then Craddock noticed the most unusual thing. All the graves were lined up, quite a few of them, small and large, but one slab was crosswise—took up three burial plots. Fred thought, "What a careless thing to do . . . maybe some disaster." About that time an old man walked up. He could tell Fred was puzzled. The man said, "I knew that fellow. We were in the same church. I knew him well, knew him all my life."

Fred asked, "Why is he buried at an angle?"

"Well, the family wanted that, and the church agreed."

"But why?"

"Cause that's the kind of guy he was. He was cross with everything. Never pleased about anything—at home or at church. He would complain, 'He's the wrong one to be doing that. I wonder who decided to do that? Why did they ask him to do that?' This is what he said all the time. The family decided that they wouldn't try to change him just because he was dead, so they buried him crosswise."

"What an awful thing to do."

"Well, they wanted it to be a witness. The family said, 'If God wants to straighten him out, God can straighten him out! But he left here just the way he lived.'"[16]

That is true for all of us. We leave here just the way we lived. Perhaps it is in the role of judge that Jesus will take on the task of straightening us out. For Christians that work begins now, when we confess that Jesus is Lord. Paul tells the church at Philippi, "that the one who began a good work among you will bring it to completion by the day of Jesus Christ" (1:6). I suspect that Paul imagined a particular time, perhaps the day of resurrection, when God would bring this work to completion. Though a "day" in biblical language may symbolically refer to an indefinite time period.

I love the story of the economist who read the passage in the Bible that says that one day with the Lord is like a thousand years to us. When the economist read that, he reasoned that time must not mean anything to God. He asked God, "God, is it true that a thousand years for us is like one minute to you?" And the Lord said, "Yes, it is true." The economist said, "Well then, is it also true that one million dollars to us is like one penny to you?" And the Lord said, "Well, yes." The economist asked, "Lord, will you give me one of those pennies?" And the Lord said, "All right, I will. Wait here—a minute." It may take a long time to straighten some of us out.

Rather than perpetuate the duality of "us" and "them" (the saved and unsaved, the righteous and wicked), each group being assigned separate destinies as is common in apocalyptic and dualistic versions of Christianity, it is more reasonable and true to the God of Jesus of Nazareth to bring judgment and salvation together as part of the total providential, redemptive, restorative, transformative work of God to reconcile all things to God's self. This perspective, grounded in a healthier, more holistic, gracious, and intellectually credible vision of God than is imagined in the traditional view of dual destinies, is not without support in the biblical tradition.

Paul responded to a situation in Corinth where some members of the faith community felt that the resurrection was limited to a spiritual experience to be enjoyed now, and not a future reality to be expected later. Paul sought to correct that view in his discussion of the resurrection

---

16. Craddock, *Craddock Stories*, 114–16.

in 1 Corinthians 15. A part of his argument related to the representative work of Christ as the head and leader of a new humanity. Since Christ was raised, so too, all those "in Christ" will follow Christ in resurrection. Paul argued that just as "all die in Adam, so all will be made alive in Christ" (1 Cor 15:22). Does "all" really mean "all"? Will all people, not just those who believe that Christ is Lord and surrender allegiance to him, but all people, even those of other religious faiths or of no faith at all, be made alive (that is, be resurrected to a new form of life) in Christ? The text suggests as much. Paul went on to argue that death will be abolished and that all things will be subjected to Christ, who will then bring all things together in God "so that God may be all in all" (1 Cor 15:25–28).

In Paul's letter to the Romans, he wrote about the disciple's representative union and identification "in Christ." He argued that Christ has become the representative leader and head of a new humanity. He declared,

> Therefore just as one man's trespass led to condemnation for all, so one man's act of righteousness leads to justification and life for all. For just as by the one man's disobedience the many were made sinners, so by the one's man's obedience the many will be made righteous . . . so that, just as sin exercised dominion in death, so grace might also exercise dominion through justification leading to eternal life through Jesus Christ our Lord. Rom 5:18–19, 21

The language is universal and all-inclusive. Through one man's disobedience many (meaning "all") were made sinners; whereas, through one man's obedience many (meaning "all") will be made righteous. In this way grace reigns; grace achieves a universal victory by bringing the "many" to "justification leading to eternal life."

In this same letter Paul envisioned the future salvation of Israel. While he recognized that the majority in Israel had rejected Jesus as their Messiah (though he argued that there has always been a believing remnant), he envisaged a time when all Israel would be saved,

> I want you to understand this mystery: a hardening has come upon part of Israel, until the full number of the Gentiles has come in. And so all Israel will be saved; as it is written, "Out of Zion will come the Deliverer; he will banish ungodliness from Jacob. And this is my covenant with them, when I take away their sins." As regards the gospel they are enemies of God for your sake; but

> as regards election they are beloved, for the sake of their ancestors; for the gifts and the calling of God are irrevocable. Just as you were once disobedient to God but have now received mercy because of their disobedience, so they have now been disobedient in order that, by the mercy shown to you, they too may now receive mercy. For God has imprisoned all in disobedience so that he may be merciful to all. Rom 11:25b–32

How God will do this Paul did not say, because he did not know. But he did believe that this was God's irrevocable promise. And Paul believed that God would keep his word. Historian and religious writer, Gary Wills has perceptively commented about Paul's view,

> The optimism about God's inclusive plan hardly reflects the dark views of election, justification, and predestination that have been wrested out of the letter to the Romans. This is a letter of consolation and reconciliation: Paul did not think in terms of individual souls damned but of the rescue of whole peoples—indeed of the whole cosmos.[17]

In Paul's letter to the church at Philippi, he quoted what many scholars believe to be an early Christ hymn, a poetic litany to Christ used in early Christian worship. Paul quoted the hymn not to establish some doctrinal or creedal point about the person of Christ, but to call the church to adopt the mindset, attitude, and basic orientation of Jesus, who gave selflessly to others, even to the point of death on a cross. Paul wrote,

> Let this mind be in you that was in Christ Jesus, who, though he was in the form of God did not regard equality with God as something to be exploited, but emptied himself, taking the form of a slave, being born in human likeness. And being found in human form, he humbled himself and become obedient to the point of death—even death on a cross. Therefore God also highly exalted him and gave him the name that is above every name, so that at the name of Jesus every knee should bend, in heaven and on earth and under the earth, and every tongue should confess that Jesus Christ is Lord to the glory of God the Father. Phil 2:5–11

Confession of Jesus Christ as Lord was a baptismal confession regarded by the early disciples as the central Messianic confession, proclaiming

---

17. Wills, *What Paul Meant*, 136.

discipleship to Jesus Christ and membership in the Messianic (church) community. This Christ hymn anticipates a universal acknowledgement/confession of Jesus as the Lord of all creation.

In the letters to the Ephesians and Colossians, Paul (or someone in the Pauline tradition) proclaimed the good news of a universal gathering up and reconciliation of all things in Christ. In Colossians, the cosmic Christ, the Christ who is the source, agent, and goal of all creation is the one in whom, through whom, and for whom God will bring all things together into one body. The writer drew from the rich tradition of wisdom in the Hebrew Bible and from other Jewish sources where wisdom is personified as *Sophia* in order to construct an exalted picture of the cosmic Christ who redeems the universe. He wrote,

> He is the image of the invisible God, the firstborn of all creation; for in him all things in heaven and on earth were created, things visible and invisible, whether thrones or dominions or rulers or powers—all things have been created through him and for him. He himself is before all things, and in him all things hold together. He is the head of the body, the church; he is the beginning of the firstborn from the dead, so that he might come to have first place in everything. For in him all the fullness of God was pleased to dwell, and through him God was pleased to reconcile to himself all things, whether on earth or in heaven, by making peace through the blood of his cross. Col 1:15–20

Here Jesus is proclaimed as the key to God's redemptive plan for the universe. God's fullness dwells in the one in whom, through whom, and for whom God will gather up to God's self all things. In this text, Jesus' nonviolent atonement, his bearing the sin (the hate and animosity) of the world in his own body on the cross, makes peace (reconciliation) the hope and prospect for the entire created universe—through his death "all things, whether on earth or in heaven" will be reconciled to God. This same idea is expounded in the letter to the Ephesians,

> With all wisdom and insight he has made known to us the mystery of his will, according to his good pleasure that he set forth in Christ, as a plan for the fullness of time, to gather up all things in him, things in heaven and things on earth. Eph 1:8b–10

God's plan, according to this passage, is in the fullness of time to gather up (reconcile) all things, in heaven and on earth (the entire created universe) in Christ. Nothing or no one is left out; all things are gathered up and brought together in Christ.

Biblical scholar and author, John Dominic Crossan has argued in his book, *God and Empire: Jesus Against Rome, Then and Now*, that in the biblical tradition, both Old and New Testaments, two incompatible and contradictory explanations of God's final victory over the evil and injustice of the world run side by side, often in the same biblical books. One explanation is extermination. It is reflected in the Noachic solution to evil in the world, namely, the complete destruction of the wicked. Crossan writes,

> In this vision, God's solution to the problem of human violence is the Great Final Battle in which good triumphs over evil—and triumphs, let us be clear, by divine violence. The symbolic place of that cosmic cleanup as cosmic slaughter is at Har Magiddo in Hebrew (hence our English "Armageddon"), the mountain pass where the spine of Israel's hill country cuts westward toward the coast and skirts a great plain suitable for battle.[18]

Examples of this approach can be found in Micah 5:15; 7:10, 16–17 and Revelation 14:20, 19:11–21.

The alternate explanation of God's final resolution to the problem of evil is reflected in the Abrahamic solution, where God calls out a people through whom he proposes to bless the world. In place of a great Final Battle to end all battles, this solution imagines a Great Final Banquet, and its symbolic place is Mount Zion. Examples of this position can be found in Micah 4:1–4, Isaiah 23:6–8, and Zechariah 8:20–23. These texts express the hope that "all peoples and nations will convert to the God of nonviolence in a world without weapons and to the God of justice in a world without empires."[19]

The two options picture God's judgment proceeding in two different directions. Is God's judgment punitive and retributive, meeting violence with violence? Or is God's judgment restorative and redemptive, responding to evil the way a loving father or mother would respond when faced with evil in one's child?

In the Gospels, Jesus speaks of judgment, but always in vague and general terms. The harsh, retributive, vengeful elements found in the judgment parables of Matthew's Gospel are most likely embellishments

18. Crossan, *God and Empire*, 83.
19. Ibid., 86.

added by Matthew and his community.[20] Jesus' portrait of a God who loves God's enemies makes it highly unlikely that extermination is God's solution to evil in the world.

What is the victory that God desires for the creation? What is the victory that Jesus' life, death, and resurrection help secure? If God really loves the world would God give up on its redemption and turn on the world so vengefully? One might imagine God simply allowing evil to exist so that it judges itself, so that it reaps what it sows, but is this the victory over evil that Jesus' death and resurrection achieves? Surely evil is exposed as evil at the cross, not simply for the purpose of revealing its true nature, but so that evil can be redeemed and won over to the good. Divine Love does not achieve victory by simply eradicating and exterminating evil, but by transforming it into something positive.

Perhaps one aspect of God's judgment involves God allowing those who have abandoned life to feel the full effects of death. In Paul's denouncement of idolatry in Romans 1:18–32, three times Paul says, "God gave them up" (1:24, 26, 28). In this passage "the wrath of God" is not a psychological evaluation of God's nature, but an expression of God's judgment, permitting human beings to reap the destruction and diminishment of life they bring on themselves when they rebel against the truth they know in their hearts.

In this text, God's judgment consists primarily of allowing those who have said "No" to the good, face the consequences of their evil. Would God, however, be a just and loving God if God permitted this state forever? Perhaps "hell" is best understood as a kind of judgment we bring on ourselves that prepares the way for our redemption.

It's not difficult to imagine how this works now, because most of us have experienced "hell" in one form or another, and it has, at times, led us back into the experience of transformative and redemptive grace. It is more difficult to imagine how this might work in a state of existence after death—in a state of existence prior to resurrection or in a resurrected state. It makes sense, however, that the process of redemption would extend beyond temporal life on earth, when one considers all the ways freedom is limited in this life through genetics, family of origins, economics, childhood experiences, education, cultural influences, and the entire socialization process.

---

20. See Queen, *The Good News According to Jesus*, 185–193.

Clarence Jordan argued, in a sermon titled, "God's Destination for Man," that this whole issue is inseparably related to the nature of God's persistent and unconditional love. Jordan asked, "How earnest, really, is his love? What kind of a God are we dealing with? This isn't just something for the theologians to debate. It really casts some light on the nature of God."[21] Jordan observed that God is not bound by time or circumstances in his relationship with humanity. He declared,

> Why should we find fault that God wants to extend the redemptive processes? Should that not be a cause of great rejoicing to us? If it's such a joy to win a soul on earth, why would it be any less of a joy to win it in the life hereafter? Would it really not be multiplied? Will we have a second chance? Of course. A third chance? Yes. A fifth chance. A thousandth chance. A millionth chance. A twin-quillion-billion-trillionth chance! For God will seek us—how long? Until he finds us. And when he's found the last little shriveling rebellious soul and has depopulated hell, then death will be swallowed up in victory, and Christ will turn over all things to the Father that he may be all in all. Then every tongue shall confess that Jesus Christ is Lord, to the glory of God the Father.[22]

The process of redemption and transformation must surely extend beyond our brief temporal existence in this life.

There is the possibility that some individuals could become so pervaded by evil that they are unredeemable, in which case, termination of life would seem logical. But grace transcends logic. It seems much more likely that the death and resurrection of Christ was meant to be a demonstration of God's ultimate victory over all rebellion and evil—an indication that God will bear the evil of creation as long as it takes to save and transform the creation. Is anyone really beyond all hope of redemption?

An experience I had early in ministry still haunts me occasionally. I was asked to perform a funeral for an alcoholic, belligerent, meanspirited man, who drank himself to death and had few friends. Only a handful of people showed up for the funeral. His sister was the only family member present. This was during a time when I still bought into most of the traditional theology of my early training. The deceased man had never made a profession of faith and while I did not put him in "hell" in

---

21. Jordan, *The Substance of Faith*, 165.
22. Ibid., 169–70.

my sermon, I certainly did not express any possibility that he might be with God. After the service the sister came up to me with a disturbed, frightened look, "Do you not offer him any hope of redemption?" At the time I could not offer her any comforting word and all I can remember is that I stumbled through some kind of response, wanting to put the whole thing behind me as soon as possible. But the question has stayed with me. Certainly today, I would have a much more hopeful message to share.

An inclusive gospel inverts our images of judgment and invests them with new meaning. The "furnace of fire" becomes a furnace that burns off all the dross, leaving the precious metal; it consumes all the selfishness and sin, so that the one who has been through the flames comes forth purged and pure. Perhaps the journey through "outer darkness" is necessary to dispel the inner darkness and illumine our minds and hearts to the mystery, wonder, and power of God's goodness and grace. Maybe the "weeping and gnashing of teeth" is a necessary prelude to the joy and celebration that results from the experience of grace and real gratitude.

Paul writes in his letter to the Corinthians,

> Love is patient . . . Love never ends. But as for prophecies, they will come to an end; as for tongues, they will cease; as for knowledge, it will come to an end. For we know only in part, and we prophesy only in part; but when the complete comes, the partial will come to an end. When I was a child, I spoke like a child, I thought like a child, I reasoned like a child; when I became an adult, I put an end to childish ways. For now we see in a mirror, dimly, but then we will see face to face. Now I know only in part; then I will know fully, even as I have been fully known. And now faith, hope, and love abide, these three; and the greatest of these is love." 1 Cor 13: 4, 8–13

If God's love never ends and if Jesus' nonviolent atonement—his bearing the hate, wrath, and cruelty of the world upon himself in order to absorb it and transform it—reflects Gods loving patience and the extent to which God is willing to go to redeem the creation, then God will surely do whatever is necessary to rescue those who have gone astray and put to right that which has gone awry.

The journey of personal redemption is a journey from the selfish ways of childhood to the adulthood of self-giving love. It is a journey from the partial to the complete, from immaturity to maturity, from brokenness to wholeness, and from the false self to the true self. I believe that it is a journey that every human being will make. Each journey is unique. Each journey has its own twists and turns, setbacks and advances, defeats and victories.

I love the story about a colony of grubs that lived at the bottom of a swamp. Occasionally, one of them would get the urge to swim to the surface and disappear, never to be heard from again. Whenever this happened the others would question and wonder among themselves. One day they decided to enter an agreement. The next one in their colony that felt the urge to leave would return and tell the others what it's like above the surface of the water. It wasn't long before one of them felt the need to depart. She swam to the surface, crawled out onto a lily pad and in the warmth of the sun went to sleep. As she slept the carapace of that little creature broke apart and out emerged this beautiful, rainbow colored dragonfly. Soon she was soaring above the waters, taking in the beauty of a bright, new world. Then, for a moment, she was sad as she remembered the promise she had made to the other grubs. But the sadness was quickly exchanged for joy when she realized that they too would make the journey, they too would experience the glory.

I believe that all will make the journey. It will be different for each of us, and there may be many experiences of "hell" before we reach "heaven," before the partial becomes complete, but the one who began the good work will surely bring it to completion.

THE COSMIC CHRIST AND OTHER RELIGIONS

What about adherents and practitioners of other religious traditions? How are they made complete? Will it be through Christ or some other means? I cannot endorse the thinking that all religious roads lead to God, but I do believe that God will travel down any road to get to us. God is surely able to accommodate God's self to our limited, inaccurate, even distorted and unhealthy images and beliefs about God in order to draw us to God's self.

The Rev Peter Gomes wrote about the time he was on a panel with Rick Warren, mega-church pastor of Saddleback Church in California and author of the book, *The Purpose-Driven Life* that has sold millions of copies. He jokingly said to Rev Warren that he was guilty of the sins of envy and covetousness—for he envied his sales and coveted his royalties.

Rev Gomes quiped, "He took the remark in good humor, as he could well afford to do." They were asked a variety of questions, but one question the interrogators particularly focused on was whether anyone can be saved who is not a born-again Christian. Gomes observed, "Rick's answer was as generous as his theology would allow, but the crux of the matter for him were the words in John's Gospel, 'I am the way, the truth, and the life; no man cometh unto the Father but by me'" (John 14:6). When Rev Warren threw the smoldering potato over to Rev Gomes, Rev Gomes replied that he could not imagine that the God who is the creator of all would have no plan of salvation for the billions of others in the world, and perhaps even beyond our galaxy, except the New Testament one. "Surely," answered Gomes, "God has not forgotten those of his creation who are not Christians. Romans tells us that he certainly has not forgotten the Jews." Then he turned toward Rev Warren and declared, "So, Rick, I can only conclude that my God is bigger than yours."[23]

God is certainly more gracious, compassionate, and generous than any of us would ever think about being. We all fail to live up to our best visions, but an interesting phenomena is that some persons, while clinging to dualistic beliefs, rise above them in their actual experience. For example, in light of Rev Warren's theology, his endorsement of Rabbi David J. Wolpe's book, *Why Faith Matters*, is both fascinating and hopeful. Warren wrote in the Foreword,

> The closer I get to David Wolpe, the more I am impressed by this man of faith. As an author, religious teacher, professor, cancer victim, and television commentator, his unique contribution of experiences has given him a credible platform from which he presents the case that faith in God truly matters at this critical time in our world. Regardless of where you are on your own personal faith journey, I'm certain that the profound insights in this book will stimulate your thinking and even touch your soul about the reality of God in fresh and surprising ways.[24]

The reason this endorsement is so intriguing is that, according to Warren's theology, Rabbi Wolpe is not "saved"—he doesn't know Jesus Christ as his personal savior, he hasn't been born again—which means (in traditional evangelical teaching) that he is not destined for heaven and is under the condemnation of God. Here is an example of a promi-

---

23. Gomes, *The Scandalous Gospel of Jesus*, 40–41.
24. Wolpe, *Why Faith Matters*, x.

nent evangelical leader, who, though still clinging to a dualistic theology, has emotionally, spiritually, and psychologically outgrown it.

Harvard religion professor, Diana Eck has been lecturing and writing for some time on the religious diversity in America. In an interview with Bob Abernethy, she mentioned an elderly friend in India who asked her once, "Do you really believe that God came only once, so very long ago and only to one people?" Professor Eck told Abernethy, "The very idea that God could be so stingy as to show up only once, to one people, in one part of the world exploded my understanding of incarnation."[25]

In the same interview, she told the story of a Vietnamese Buddhist temple in Boston, where the image of the bodhisattva (enlightened being) of compassion, named Quan Yen, was smashed by some boys from the projects next door. When the vandals were caught, instead of taking the boys to court, the Vietnamese Buddhists forgave them. They had a festival of forgiveness and invited the whole neighborhood. They displayed an ethic of love and forgiveness that most Christians would cherish. Professor Eck talked with one of the vandals named Angelo. When the president of the temple welcomed him the morning of the festival the president said, "Your name means angel; we're going to make you and your friends the guardian angels of the temple." Angelo later said to Professor Eck, "If I had known anything about this temple and these people I would never have done this."[26]

Certainly Christians do not have a corner on the knowledge or grace of God. God transcends our limited categories of understanding and cannot be fully expressed by our language or confined to our confessional statements.

We come to know God through both understanding and experience, which are always limited. In the story of the call of Moses, God appeared to him "in a flame of fire out of a bush" (Ex. 3:2). When Moses inquired as to God's name, trying to understand God and wanting to explain God's identity to his people, God responded, "I am who I am" (Ex. 3:14). This ambiguous response communicates mystery and conveys a sense of wonder. Why? Because a name cannot capture God; God can go by many names. To define God by a name would be to confine God to a particular expression of God's self.

---

25. Abernethy and Bole, *The Life of Meaning*, 337.
26. Ibid., 341.

Later in the story, Moses asks to see (experience) God's glory (Ex. 33:18). In the interchange between them God says, "And while my glory passes by I will put you in a cleft of the rock, and I will cover you with my hand until I have passed by; then I will take away my hand, and you shall see my back; but my face shall not be seen" (Ex 33:22-23). This, most likely, is the biblical writer's way of saying that we can only "see in part." Our experience of God is always limited, because God is inexhaustible and cannot be fully grasped or experienced by any creature.

Samir Selmanovic has written a wonderful book titled, *It's Really All About God: Reflections of a Muslim Athiest Jewish Christian*. He shares how his parents tried everything within their power to turn him away from Christianity soon after he embraced the Christian faith. They recruited one of Europe's best psychiatrists and over fifty relatives to take their best shot in helping their son get over his infatuation with God. Even his former girlfriends "were summoned to try to evoke sweet memories" and win his heart. While his parents were not religious, their background was Muslim and on one occasion they invited Imam Muhammad, a man respected in the Muslim community of their city, to their house to talk with Samir. His parents figured Islam was the lesser of two evils.

Samir says that Muhammad "was the most environmentally progressive and socially conscious person" he had ever met. He was a vegan who walked to his house from the other side of the city, avoiding transportation on principle in order to protect the environment. He was a small gray-haired man with a large smile emanating peace and playfulness.

Samir was expecting some sort of talk on the evils of Christianity and the superiority of Islam and the Quran. Instead, after some initial small talk, Imam Muhammad let time pass in silence. When he could tell that Samir was ready, Muhammad stood quietly, walked over to Samir, sat down, and lightly touched his shoulder for a moment. Then he said calmly, "I am glad you are a believer." And nothing more.

After sitting in peace for a little longer they stood up, and Muhammad opened his arms to invite an embrace. Samir opened his. Samir writes, "He smelled like wooden furniture and soap—old but fresh. Hugging him, I thanked God for giving me this break in life."

Samir had been converted into a conservative version of Christianity, so neither he nor his parents knew how to interpret what had just happened. Samir's parents nicknamed the imam "Crazy Muhammad" and word of his foolishness spread in the family. Reflecting on that experience Samir observes, "The grace and truth I had first met at the cross were embodied in this man, who was willing to be taken for a fool in order to make me whole."[27]

While Muhammad undoubtedly held certain beliefs central to Islam, he also believed that God was much greater than his religion, so he was able to embrace Samir as his brother. Muhammad personally knew a God who was much larger than any particular way of imagining God. He knew that if he helped foster an image of God who withholds God's self from people outside one's particular religion, he would not only make God less than Divine, he would make God less than human.

Too many Christians imagine a God who is less than human. Isn't it time we grow up? Isn't it time to let go of the divisive notion that we must convert people of other religious faiths to our way of knowing and serving God? Surely the time has come for Christians to let go of images of God that contribute to a divided, polarized and conflicted world.

The exclusive language in the Bible is understandable given the milieu in which Christianity was born. Before Christianity spread into the Roman world, the first followers of Jesus were Jews; the Jesus movement began as a Jewish reform movement. These first Jewish disciples were immersed in an apocalyptic imagination and worldview that had come to prevail in Jewish communities a couple of centuries before and after Christ. This worldview was the natural development of a dispossessed people struggling for a sense of identity with a minority faith; a people who frequently encountered oppression and opposition from the larger society. Apocalyptic images of vindication fostered an exclusive point of reference and orientation that distinguished between those on the inside (us) and those on the outside (them). Christians who take the Bible literally tend to focus on passages in the New Testament that reflect this limited and narrow perspective. Though dualistic language is common biblical language, there is also, as I presented previously, a strong trajectory in the biblical tradition toward a more inclusive and universal faith perspective.

One passage drawn from the basket of exclusive texts is found in Acts 4. According to Luke, Peter and John were taken into custody by the Jewish leaders and called to give an account of their preaching and healing in the name of Jesus. In the context of claiming healing power through the resurrected Christ, Peter says, "There is salvation in no one else, for there is no other name under heaven given among mortals by

27. Selmanovic, *It's Really All About God*, 84–88.

The Triumph of Love   113

which we must be saved" (Acts 4:12). The "we" in the text is a reference to his fellow Jews. Peter proclaims Jesus to be Israel's Messiah; that God's redemptive plan for Israel now finds its fulfillment in the life, death, and resurrection of Jesus. There is no reason to interpret this as an exclusive claim that persons who do not know Jesus cannot be accepted before God. A later text in Acts points the reader toward a more universal perspective.

In Acts 10, Peter receives a vision in which he is instructed to eat meat prohibited in the Levitical code. Peter, a good Jew, objects, "By no means, Lord; for I have never eaten anything that is profane or unclean" (Acts 10:14). The voice responds, "What God has made clean, you must not call profane" (Acts 10:15).

Peter finds himself in the home of the Gentile Cornelius, a Roman centurion. Cornelius, too, has had a vision and when Peter hears it he is given a new insight. Peter concludes, "I truly understand that God shows no partiality, but in every nation anyone who fears him and does what is right is acceptable to him" (10:34–35). Peter comes to an extremely inclusive position, not by rationalization, but by revelation. Peter's eyes are opened. He now has a much bigger God. A God not only of the Jews, but of all people.

Peter goes on to share the particulars of the Christian faith—the life, death, and resurrection of Christ. While Peter proclaims to them the good news of Christ, the Spirit comes upon all gathered in that place, evidenced by the gift of tongues. Then Cornelius and his household are baptized. This passage affirms that all who "fear [which in this context means, 'respect, trust, revere'] God and do what is right" are accepted by God, even though Christian faith asserts certain particulars.

These Scripture passages in Acts may suggest that Christians in the Lukan community were struggling with both exclusive and inclusive positions. They proclaimed boldly the life, death, and resurrection of Jesus as the fulfillment of God's redemptive plan for Israel and as good news that reached beyond Israel to include Gentiles, while also recognizing that people outside their particular faith community could be accepted before God.

The text so often cited by exclusivists is John 14:6 (the passage referenced by Rev Warren mentioned earlier) where Jesus is purported as saying, "I am the way, and the truth, and the life. No one comes to the Father except through me." The Gospel of John reflects what the church in Asia at the end of the first century or the beginning of the second century had come to believe about Jesus. The discourses of Jesus in John are much more reflective of the faith and theology of the Johannine community (church) than representative of the actual words and sayings of Jesus. This means that it is extremely difficult to determine what Jesus may have actually said. Therefore, the exclusive language attributed to Jesus in John does not represent what Jesus literally said, but what the church in Asia was saying as they struggled with what Jesus meant to them.

Jesus' response in John 14 is a pastoral response to an anxious question posed by one of his disciples, undoubtedly reflecting some of the anxiety experienced in the Johannine community. Jesus had told them that he would be leaving them, and they were anxious to know where he was going and if they could go with him. This is the language of affirmation and devotion, not propositional theology.

After the conversation between Jesus and the woman of Samaria at Jacob's well, the woman hurried back to her village and exclaimed, "Come, see a man who told me everything I ever did. Could this be the Messiah?" (John 4:29). Jesus, of course, did not literally tell her everything she ever did. But he did speak the truth and she felt as if he really knew what she was about. Her report was an overstatement, an exaggeration. She shared what she felt and experienced. Her statement was not intended to be a literal, factual affirmation. John's Gospel is the language of testimony.

When the Johannine church attributes to Jesus the saying, "no one comes to the Father except through me" they are using the language of testimony to declare what was true in their own experience. It is not a factual or literal statement that is true for all people in all places. This is how they came to know God—through Jesus, God's Son. A testimony is not a propositional theological declaration; it reflects a heart-felt experience.

Neither John's church at the end of the first century nor the church of the twenty-first century are able to determine who can or cannot know God. To use the Bible in a way that pigeonholes what God can or cannot do is to misuse the Bible. John's Gospel is known for its dualistic language, sometimes drawing a clear distinction between those who have "life" and those who do not, but even this Gospel begins with a universal emphasis on the cosmic Christ, the Word (*logos*), whose life is the "light of all people" (1:4), "the true light, which enlightens everyone" (1:9).

What are we to make of the tension between the Christian's salvific experience through Christ and the claims of those in other religious faiths who encounter and experience God through their own unique traditions? Christians experience salvation in and through the life, death, and resurrection of Christ, and while this revelation is definitive and decisive for Christians, it is not final. Persons of other religious traditions may indeed encounter God through their own teachings, myths, and traditions, and the way/s in which God communicates and reveals God's self through their traditions may be regarded as decisive and definitive for them. The uniqueness of revelation in Christ, then, is not a uniqueness that is singular, exclusive, or final, though it is definitive and decisive as a means of personal and communal transformation for disciples of Christ.

This, however, still does not resolve all the tensions. If it is true, as I have suggested, that God will reconcile all things to God's self in and through Christ, and that the living Christ is the cosmic Christ who adapts and relates to people of other faiths through their own religious mediators and traditions, then I cannot deny claiming a kind of superiority to my inclusiveness. In my belief system, Christ is the universal Lord; and while I acknowledge the legitimacy of other mediators and faith traditions they are not equal to the Christ of my faith tradition.

This raises a critical issue in terms of religious dialogue with believers of other religious faiths, namely, how much to share. This may not be a belief I will be able to share in the context of religious dialogue, at least not initially. It may be possible in time to nurture and develop the kind of friendship, admiration, and respect that will make it possible to share one's deepest faith convictions with persons of other faiths. Then again, it may not; much will depend on the nature of the group.

The inclusive position I have presented differs from the pluralist position because a true pluralist would not claim Christ as the cosmic Christ in whom and through whom all things are reconciled to God. For a true pluralist, Jesus stands on an equal footing with all the other mediators of God. It is possible, however, for an inclusivist like myself to be basically pluralistic in approach to religious dialogue.

The purpose of religious dialogue is not to argue one's faith tradition as superior to other faith traditions. The goal is to listen, learn, and share in a context of mutual respect, humility, friendship, and understanding. An inclusivist can share Jesus' revelation of God's nature, Jesus' vision of God's kingdom, and Jesus' expression of authentic humanity, without conveying an air of superiority, without suggesting that the Christian way of knowing God is better than other ways of knowing God, and without suggesting that it is actually the Spirit of Christ at work through the mediators and teachings of other religious traditions. In mutual religious dialogue, my Christian interpretation of reality is but one perspective among many perspectives. In mutual dialogue I assume a position around the table that views the Divine Reality as the sun, the source of light and life, and our diverse religious traditions as planets that orbit around the sun. In such a setting no religious tradition can claim to be the sun or to be a better planet with a closer orbit than the others. For mutual dialogue to occur, all must come to the table as equal partners. We must love and listen to each other with deep attentiveness, admiration, and appreciation for our different faith traditions. In that context it may not be appropriate to share all of my Christian convictions, but I can share many of them, while I give equal time and attention to my sisters and brothers, allowing their faith sharing to inform, test, and challenge my own.

In Matthew's Gospel, the magi from the East who come to pay homage to the Christ child serve as a poignant symbol of how an inclusive faith can function in a pluralistic world. These magi are wise men, sages, astrologers, interpreters of signs, not kings. We don't know their religion, but they are not Jewish in faith. They see a sign in the heavens pointing them to Bethlehem and the birth of one who is destined to be "King of the Jews." Whatever their religion they recognize that the truth is not limited to their own religious system. They follow the star to Bethlehem where they pay homage to the Christ child, bringing gifts of gold, frankincense, and myrrh.

Bruce Sanguin, minister of Canadian Memorial Church in Vancouver, British Columbia, has pointed out that the magi were seekers of truth wherever truth could be found. They travel to Israel to pay homage and have no need to import their unique religious beliefs. Sanguin posed the question, "What would ecumenical relations with other faiths look like if they were homage based? What would it mean for Christians to make the long journey across the strange cultural and religious landscapes bearing only gifts of respect for all that is sacred in other traditions?"[28] If we adopted this model, would this lead us away from the revelation we claim in Jesus Christ? Sanguin wrote,

> The Magi were steeped deeply enough in their own tradition that they could make a pilgrimage into another culture and religion. They enjoyed the security of their own faith system sufficiently

---

28. Sanguin, "Paying Homage," 138–39.

that they could pay homage to another . . . I believe that the deeper we go into our own faith system, the closer we get to God, the more we are informed by values of diversity, inclusivity, and respect for the inherent dignity of other people and faith.[29]

I have certainly found this to be true in my own experience. Over the years I have dug deep into my Christian faith tradition, and the deeper I go the more open, inclusive, and understanding I have become toward other faith traditions. What would our Christian witness look like if our missionaries entered other cultures ready to receive as much as they give, to meet people of other faith traditions as mutual friends and pilgrims on a journey from whom they can learn, without feeling the need to convert them to their own faith system?

Dr. Fred Craddock has shared about the time he went back to west Tennessee where he was raised. While visiting, he went with a friend to his church, a small church that had new stained glass windows—expensive windows. As Craddock stood there wondering how they could possibly have afforded such windows, he began reading the dedications and didn't recognize any of the names.

He said to his friend, "Are these new people who have come in? I don't understand this; I don't recognize any of these new strange names."

His friend said, "No, a church in St. Louis ordered these windows from Italy, and when they got them, they didn't fit. They advertised in a church paper that they would sell them because they were going to have new ones made. They were so cheap we bought them."

Fred said, "Well, they sure are beautiful, but what are you going to do about the plaques?"

He said, "Well, the board discussed that, and we decided to leave those names up there. It's good for us in our little church to realize that there are some Christian people besides us."[30]

That's good, but we can go farther out. It's good for us who are Christians, in our little part of the world, to realize that God has many daughters and sons besides us.

---

29. Ibid., 140.
30. Craddock, *Craddock Stories*, 138.

4

Living the Faith

IN THE MOVIE, *CHARIOTS of Fire*, winning was everything to British runner Harold Abrams. For the first time in his life he loses a race to Eric Liddell, the Scottish champion. The pain of the loss is so overwhelming he considers not running again.

His girlfriend, Cybil, says, "Harold, this is absolutely ridiculous. It's a race you have lost, not a relative. Nobody's dead."

Harold moans, "I've lost"

"I know. I was there. I remember watching you; it was marvelous. You were marvelous. He was more marvelous, that's all. On that day the best man won. . . . He was ahead, there was nothing you could have done. He won fair and square."

"Well, that's that," Abrams says.

"If you can't take a beating, perhaps it's for the best."

"I don't run to take beatings—I run to win!" Harold screams. "If I can't win, I won't run."

Cybil pauses, and then says firmly, "If you don't run, you can't win."[1]

Races are meant to be run; Christianity is meant to be lived.

AN INVITATION TO DISCIPLESHIP

Pastor and Bible teacher, Stuart Briscoe told about teaching a New Members Class at his church. When he walked into the room for the first class, he noticed that everyone seemed extremely stiff and detached. All the participants were carefully dressed, sitting somewhat solemnly and expressionless, with one exception. Sitting on the floor in blue jeans

---

1. Referenced in Ortburg, *If You Want to Walk on Water*, 147.

with her legs crossed was a young woman. In order to break the ice he asked everyone to share a little about themselves. The first person identified himself by what he did vocationally and everyone else followed suit: "I'm a teacher"; "I'm a lawyer"; "I'm an auto mechanic"; "I'm this, I'm that." When they finally got around to the girl who was sitting on the floor, with a spark in her eye she declared, "I am a disciple of Jesus Christ cleverly disguised as a machine operator."

How many Christians, when asked to share a few significant things about themselves, would begin by saying, "I'm a disciple of Jesus Christ"? Luke's version of the call of Simon to follow Jesus can be read as a challenge to consider the practical implications of Christian discipleship (Luke 5:1–11).

The story of Peter's call to discipleship includes a fish story. A lady told her neighbor about her first fishing trip with her husband. She said, "Oh, I did everything wrong. I was too noisy. I used the wrong bait. I reeled it in too soon, and—I caught more fish than he did!" Peter was a seasoned fisherman, but this was certainly an unusual catch of fish. When Jesus, using Peter's boat as a floating platform from which to speak, finished teaching the people, he instructed Peter to row out into deeper water and let down his net. Peter was reluctant. He had been fishing all night and caught nothing. Fishing was done primarily at night because there was less possibility of spooking the fish. The fish were not running and now it is daylight, and Jesus tells him to try again. This may have initially seemed to Peter to be a sure waste of time, ridiculous really, but it was Jesus who spoke the word, and there was something compelling about Jesus and the ring of authority in his voice. "Because *you say so*, I will let down the nets" (Luke 5:5, emphasis mine).

Peter acts in faith. He acts on the word of Jesus, not on the reasonableness or logic of the command. That is not to say that reason and logic are unimportant. Christian faith is not blind faith, devoid of reason, logic, or intellectual credibility. These elements of faith keep faith from becoming mere fantasy or illusion. Faith, however, cannot be proved. It cannot be reduced to a definition, thesis, or scientific formula.

Faith is rooted in real life experience. There was something about Jesus that evoked confidence. Peter certainly would have not responded as he did if someone less compelling than Jesus had issued the instruction. Peter, though undoubtedly hesitant and reluctant, felt compelled to obey the command of Jesus. A life of discipleship begins when one is bold enough to act in faith on the word of Christ.

It's interesting that Jesus calls Peter, not in a synagogue, employing religious or theological language, but on a lake, where Peter was most at home. Jesus meets Peter on his turf (or surf). Could it be that the living Christ looks for opportunities to reveal God to us in the world where we live and work?

Bruce Larson shared about a friend who worked as a chief engineer at a laboratory that produced sound equipment. They had received a custom order for two hundred amplifiers and when they all came off the assembly line none of them worked. They checked all the blueprints, then all the parts, and could find nothing wrong. The engineer went into his office and prayed, "Lord, what is wrong with these amplifiers?" As he was praying, an idea popped into his mind to cross two particular wires. It didn't quite make sense to do it, but when he tried it, it worked. When he shared this experience with his prayer group he said, "Jesus was showing me that he knew more about electronics than I did."

Was it the living Christ? There's no way to validate or invalidate his conclusion. It cannot be scientifically investigated or challenged, but he believed that he had heard the voice of the living Christ. His prayer may have been more desperation than faith, but in his experience Christ met him where he was and compelled him to trust him.

What is it that one must believe in order to be a follower of Jesus? If this text in any way provides a pattern for discipleship or even an illustration of it, then conformity to doctrinal fundamentals, theological propositions, or statements of belief is not a requisite. It is not even mandatory that one believe "that Jesus died for our sins in accordance with the scriptures, and that he was buried, and that he was raised on the third day in accordance with the scriptures" (1 Cor 15:3–4). The early Christians did indeed believe this tradition that Paul says he "had received" from those who were disciples before him. But even belief in this early formulation of the death and resurrection of Jesus is not necessary in order to begin the journey of discipleship. What is necessary, however, is some degree of confidence that the way of Jesus leads to an authentic human existence personally, relationally, and communally.

Immediately prior to the public teaching of Jesus from the boat and the call of Peter, Luke's Gospel has a short description of what Jesus was preaching and teaching. Jesus had withdrawn from the crowd in solitude to pray. The people found him, and when they realized that he was planning to move on, tried to prevent him. But he said, "I must proclaim the kingdom of God to the other cities also; for I was sent for this purpose" (Luke 4:43). Here, as I discussed in chapter 2, Jesus defines his mission in terms of the kingdom of God—God's new world of peace and righteousness, of reconciled relationships and a renewed earth, of distributive justice and abounding grace.

This is what Peter would have heard—the good news of God's plan for a healed and transformed world. At this juncture in his spiritual journey, however, Peter would have had a somewhat limited and inaccurate understanding of the nature and dynamics of the kingdom of God, though he would in time come to share Jesus' vision. Peter trusted Jesus and his cause, whatever that cause would entail. He was willing to make the necessary investment and sacrifice in order to be one of Jesus' disciples.

A pastor was officiating at the funeral of a war veteran. The deceased man's military friends wanted to have a part in the service at the funeral home, so they asked the pastor to lead them to the casket, stand with them in a solemn moment of remembrance, and then lead them out through the side door. This, the pastor proceeded to do, though the effect was somewhat marred when he picked the wrong door. In full view of the mourners they marched with military precision right into a broom closet, from which they had to make an embarrassing retreat.

The most important consideration in discipleship is that the person one chooses to follow knows where he or she is going. The first disciples of Jesus trusted that he would lead them in the way of truth. They were known as people "who belonged to the Way" (Acts 9:2).

Jesus' first disciples were attracted to and compelled to follow him because . . . we don't know for certain. Was it his charismatic personality? His authoritative teaching? His vision of a new world? His capacity to heal and drive out evil spirits? His compassion for the poor and oppressed? His intimacy with God and immersion in God's Spirit? Perhaps for some or all of these reasons the first disciples felt compelled to leave their livelihoods, their families, and their communities in order to embark upon the risky adventure of learning from Jesus how to live, love, and serve others in the world.

When Peter and those with him let down their nets at the command of Jesus, Luke says that they caught so many fish that their nets started to break. So they recruited assistance from their partners close at hand to help them land the catch.

For Peter, this experience became a revelation of Jesus' uniqueness as a special agent and mediator of the redemptive presence and power of God. Luke says, "He fell down at Jesus' knees, saying, 'Go away from me, Lord, I am a sinful man'" (Luke 5:8). Sin, as depicted here, is not so much moral inferiority as it is distance from God (perceived, not actual distance). Whenever we touch the reality of God, whenever God breaks through our illusions and defenses, and becomes known to us (this is always an imperfect knowledge), we immediately sense how "small" we are in light of the "largeness" of God. Some immediately feel embraced by God's unconditional love; others feel distance, like Peter in this story. Everyone's experience is unique.

This was not a conversion experience in the sense that Peter was converted from Judaism to Christianity. Peter, a Jew, recognizes in the Jewish Jesus a person immersed in God's Spirit and a mediator of the Divine. Peter trusts Jesus as one who knows and reveals God. Nor is this a conversion experience in the sense that Peter was converted from the mere formality of religion to a personal relationship with God. We do not know how Peter experienced God prior to his encounter with Jesus. For all we know, Peter may have not felt any distance from God at all prior to this encounter.

Peter's discipleship to Jesus becomes a new stage in his life of faith, and through this relationship Peter will be changed. He will undergo a process of conversion from that of a basically self-centered individual into a more loving, self-giving person, who in time, will come to share Jesus' vision of a redeemed world.

It seems that a basic principle of the spiritual life is that the closer we draw toward God or are drawn toward God (God is the initiator), the more insight and illumination we are given regarding the character of God and what it means to live an authentic human life. Any number of experiences can make us aware of our need for divine grace. Even those of us who place a priority on our relationship with God, may sense at any time our need for God's wisdom, love, and passion for justice.

Many authentic experiences of God occur at the point where we confront the truth about our greed, egoism, and selfish ambition. When God's Spirit pierces our carefully self-constructed layers of ego protection and shatters our illusions about who we are, we tend to feel a profound and heavy sense of unworthiness. We can't live here, but it is likely that we all must pass through this place at least once (perhaps many times) on our spiritual journeys. When grace penetrates our defenses and we experience God's acceptance and unconditional love, gratitude wells up within us like living water.

As important as such experiences are, however, the invitation to discipleship is not mainly about transcendent encounters. It is an invitation to nurture a relationship with Jesus Christ that involves trust in and commitment to the cause of Jesus and the things he cares about. (I intentionally use the present tense here because discipleship to Jesus involves, not only a commitment to teaching once delivered, but the present dynamic of following the Spirit of the living Christ).

Jesus calls disciples to a relationship that demands our fullest attention and deepest devotion. Bobby Bowden, who for years was the widely celebrated football coach of Florida State University, was known for his propensity to tell stories to motivate his players. One story Bowden is noted for is a baseball story. He played baseball in college and had never hit a home run. In one at bat, he hit a shot over the first base bag that went all the way to the wall. As he rounded second, the coach waved him around third to score, for an inside the park home run. He was excited and his teammates were slapping him fives. But then the pitcher took the ball, threw it to the first baseman (touching the bag), and the umpire called him out. He had missed first base. In sharing this story with Christian groups Bowden says, "If you don't take care of first base, it doesn't matter what else you do. Nothing else really matters if you do not honor the Lord first."

I cannot concur with the absoluteness of his conclusion, but I recognize the legitimacy of the basic point he is making. The first thing that is foundational to the life of Christian discipleship is confidence in and commitment to Jesus as Lord. Not in the doctrinal sense of adhering to a particular belief (or beliefs) about the nature of Jesus, but in the practical sense of faithfulness to the way of life Jesus embodied and taught.

In the ancient world discipleship was not uncommon. Various groups attracted disciples. The rabbis and teachers of the law enlisted disciples responsible for learning and passing on their oral traditions and interpretations. The Greek philosophers attracted disciples to assimilate and propagate their philosophies. It was not that unusual for Jesus to call disciples. Jesus, however, gathered disciples to join him in announcing in word and deed the good news of God's new world, and to learn from him how to be God's agents and emissaries in its creative realization (Luke 5:10).[2]

Discipleship to Christ, then, is a relationship that leads to partnership in Christ's cause, which is the kingdom of God. As I argued in chapter 2, Jesus understood his mission in terms of proclaiming, teaching, and manifesting the kingdom of God—God's new world (Luke 4:43). When Jesus said to Peter and the other fishermen, "from now on you will be catching people," Jesus was not articulating a mandate for a triumphalistic missionary enterprise that seeks to impose a particular culture and set of beliefs on people of a different culture and set of beliefs.

It is unfortunate that traditional Christianity, as practiced by the majority of Christians in the Western world, has understood the church's mission to be one of spreading Christendom, which has often sought to dominate and domesticate other faiths and cultures. This approach has done enormous harm in our world, especially when evangelistic efforts have been wedded to the imperialistic ideals of our nation and Western society. Adherents of this approach measure the success of their ventures, not in terms of faithfulness to a way of life devoted to the genuine good of others, but in terms of how many souls are won to imperialistic Christendom (usually reported as souls saved).

The kind of fishing for people that Jesus expected his disciples to do was the kind he himself practiced. Disciples of Jesus learn from Jesus what to do and how to do it. Jesus' mission, as Luke outlines in 4:18–19 (grounded in Isaiah 61:1–2) was a mission to the poor, the disadvantaged, the oppressed, and the spiritually blind. Disciples share in this mission through concrete, tangible acts of mercy and justice on behalf of the poor and oppressed, as they embody an ethic of divine love (*agape*).

Catching people in the net of God's rule (of divine love) does not necessarily mean catching them into the net of the church. The church is not the kingdom, though the church (as I explained in chapter 2) is called to be an outpost for the kingdom. The kingdom, however, is much broader and wider than the church.

The kingdom of God as it pertains to humanity is about human beings becoming more truly human. It is not about propagating a particular brand of Christian belief or doctrine. Jesus as "the Son of Man" is the representative, revelatory human being on 'being human." Jesus

---

2. See Luke 9:1–6 and 10:1–20.

Living the Faith 125

as "the Word (*Logos*) made flesh" incarnates the divine (or the truly human). For Christians, he is the primary symbol, the archetype of what it means to reflect the image of God in flesh and blood.

Is not the kingdom of God as envisioned by Jesus much greater than what Christendom has traditionally imagined? Disciples of Jesus are apprentices of Jesus, who seek first the kingdom of God by immersion in the divine love that Jesus so beautifully incarnated.

The mission of the church, then, is to proclaim, teach, manifest, and creatively participate in the kingdom of God on earth, not coerce people to believe what they believe about Jesus or force others to adopt their particular Christian practices and rituals. Christians with a kingdom vision invite others to be disciples of Jesus because they know that by following Jesus God's dream for the world can be realized, and they naturally want others to experience the abundant life they have discovered in their discipleship to Jesus.

LIVING AN ABUNDANT LIFE

The late theological educator and spiritual writer, Henry Nouwen described life in the world as both filled and unfulfilled.[3] Our lives are filled with things to do, people to meet, projects to finish, appointments to keep; they are like overpacked suitcases bursting at the seams. We are bombarded with life's demands and opportunities. And yet, says Nouwen, our lives remain unfulfilled. While our minds and hearts are filled with many things, there exists a nagging sense of unfulfillment. While busy and hurried, we seldom feel truly satisfied and at peace. The result of all this overstimulation is that we get caught in a web of false expectations and contrived needs that often leave us feeling bored, anxious, fearful, and depressed. The great paradox of our day is that while our lives are filled with so many things, we still feel unfulfilled; we sense that something is missing.

There was a preacher who liked to read and preach from a big loose leaf Bible. One Sunday he preached from the Genesis text about Adam and Eve. As he stood up to preach, unnoticed by him, one of his pages fell out. He was reading along, "And Adam said to Eve," and he turned the page. He paused and read again, "And Adam said to Eve." He looked under his Bible as he said again, "And Adam said to Eve . . . very in-

---

3. Nouwen, *Making All Things New*, 23–37.

teresting, looks like a leaf is missing." Often our filled, but unfulfilled lives will leave us with a sense that something profound and important is missing.

In John 10:10 Jesus says, "The thief comes only to steal and kill and destroy. I came that they may have life, and have it abundantly." This statement of purpose occurs in the discourse of the shepherd and sheep in John 10:1-18. The sheepfold figures prominently in this imagery. The sheepfold is an enclosed area with a single opening. It could be located in the open country or attached to a house. The shepherd leads his flock through the opening (the gate) into the sheepfold to protect them from thieves and predators. He leads them out to find pasture. The sheep recognize the voice of the shepherd and follow along behind as he leads them in and out.

While the basic imagery is simple, the structure of the text in John 10 is rather complex. Jesus is pictured as both the gate and the shepherd. The two parables (some scholars would not call these parables) are combined in John 10:1-5. The first parable (10:1-3a) involves the gate and is interpreted in 10:7-10. The second parable (10:3b-5) relates to the shepherd and is interpreted in 10:11-16.

It is difficult to know how much of this, if any, goes back to Jesus. It is likely that the images of the gate and the shepherd originated with Jesus, though it would be sheer conjecture to reconstruct what Jesus may have actually said. Jesus may have employed these images to talk about the disciple's relationship to God and to one another in the faith community. In the developing thought and faith of the early church, the disciple's relationship to Jesus became the equivalent of the disciple's relationship to God.

Jesus, the good shepherd, is contrasted with thieves and bandits (undoubtedly an allusion to the opponents of Jesus), and with hired hands (perhaps a reference to religious teachers who were mainly interested in their own advancement and glory). The tone of the passage, however, is much more pastoral than it is polemical. The passage has less to do with Jesus' opponents and more to do with the relationship of the disciples to Jesus.

The promise of fullness/abundance of life must be understood in connection with other texts on discipleship that forewarn of the trouble and hardship disciples encounter. In John 16:33 Jesus says to the disciples, "In the world you face persecution. But take courage; I have conquered the world." There is a paradoxical tension in these texts that is not easily or simply resolved. They seem to imply that disciples can experience a fullness of life in relationship with Christ while also facing opposition and persecution from the powers that be.

The abundance or fullness of life that is mentioned in 10:10 defines what the writer means by "saved" in 10:9, "Whoever enters by me will be saved, and will come in and go out and find pasture." The imagery speaks of a flourishing life. One might think of the imagery from the twenty-third Psalm, "The Lord is my shepherd, I shall not want. He makes me lie down in green pastures; he leads me beside still waters; he restores my soul" (Ps 23:1–3). To be saved, according to Jesus/John in this particular context, involves a flourishing life in Christ.

In John's Gospel "death" and "life" are poignant, theologically packed religious symbols. Death represents the absence of spiritual life. In a contemporary spiritual sense, it may be symbolic of the darkness of depression; or the enmity, estrangement, and alienation that separates individuals from one another and from their true selves; or a felt absence of love, meaning, and significance.

Life, the antithesis of death, is what one experiences in relationship with God. In a contemporary existential sense, it may stand as a symbol for relationships and experiences that are healthy, vibrant, holistic, and transformative. Life involves freedom from the debilitating power of anxiety, worry, and fear. Life reflects the love, joy, and peace experienced by an individual or faith community when that person or community is delivered from the oppressive power of hate, guilt, and shame.

Life is what happens to us when we open our hearts to the love of God and decide to share and express God's love to others. Death is what happens to us when we close our hearts to God's love and decide instead to harbor resentment and animosity.

There is an obvious contrast in the shepherd and sheep discourse between Jesus' care for the sheep as the good shepherd and the lack of care exhibited by the thieves and the hired hands (John 10:10–15). The good shepherd knows the sheep by name and they know him, but the hired hand does not know them or care for them. The hired hands and thieves look after themselves; they care nothing for the sheep. The good shepherd, however, is willing to lay down his life for the sheep. Anyone who desires to enter into the abundant life made available in Jesus must experience and reflect to some degree the love and care that

Jesus demonstrated as the good shepherd. One who is self-centered and predominately self-occupied cannot experience the kind of fullness of life this Gospel speaks about.

One, of course, has to take care of one's self. A balance is necessary. In order to love others as I love myself, I must love myself. If I do not love myself, I will be incapable of loving others. If I completely neglect my own needs in the service of others, I am not likely to experience the flourishing life of Jesus. Self-neglect and self-rejection can be just as diminishing and detrimental to the spiritual life as self-centeredness and self-aggrandizement. A deflated ego can have the same effect as an inflated ego.

In the imagery developed by John/Jesus much is made of the sheep listening to the voice of the good shepherd and the good shepherd going before them and the sheep following. The sheep do not listen to the voice of the stranger, who does not care for them; they listen to the good shepherd who is even willing to lay down his life for their protection and benefit (10:4–5, 14–15).

In the context of the Johannine community, this was experienced, as we experience such leading today, through the Spirit. Jesus says to his disciples,

> I will not leave you orphaned; I am coming to you. In a little while the world will no longer see me, but you will see me; because I live, you also will live . . . I have said these things to you while I am still with you. But the Advocate, the Holy Spirit, whom the Father will send in my name, will teach you everything, and remind you of all that I have said to you. John 14:18, 25–26

Jesus says that the Spirit will guide them into the truth that Jesus embodied and revealed (John 16:13); that the Spirit will take what is his and reveal it to the disciples (John 16:14).

The voice of the Spirit is the voice of Jesus. The living Christ speaks to his disciples by means of the Spirit and his disciples learn to discern and follow his voice by listening to the voice of the Spirit.

Two men were walking down a busy street in New York City. One stopped suddenly and said, "I hear a cricket." His friend scoffed, "How in the world can you hear a cricket in all this noise?" The first man explained that he was a naturalist and was trained to hear crickets. To prove his point, he reached in his pocket and took out a fifty-cent piece and dropped it on the pavement. Several people stopped and looked down. We tend to hear what has meaning for us.

Certainly the Spirit speaks to us individually as we read and reflect on Scripture and other spiritual writings, as we pray, study, and quiet our lives through solitude and silence. Equally important, however, is the way the Spirit speaks to us in community—in corporate worship, instruction, prayer, fellowship, and in ministry together. The early disciples believed that the living Christ was present in their communal life in ways and means that would not have been available to them in isolation from the community.

Do we really believe that when two or three of us gather in the name of Christ, his living presence is among us (Matt 18:20)? Do we come together expecting to hear the voice of the Good Shepherd? We need the community to help us hear the voice of Christ, who speaks to us from deep within our true self.

Parker Palmer related how he took a yearlong sabbatical from his work in Washington D. C. to go to Pendle Hill, a Quaker living-and-learning community of some seventy people, outside of Philadelphia. Their mission, explained Parker, is to offer education about the inner, spiritual journey, nonviolent social change, and the relationship between the two. Their communal life involved worship in silence each morning, shared meals, study, physical work, decision making, and social outreach. During Palmer's tenure as dean at Pendle Hill, he was offered the opportunity to become president of a small educational institution. He visited the campus, spoke with administrators, trustees, faculty, and students, and had been basically told that the job was his if he wanted it.

Though he felt quite certain this was the job for him, in the Quaker tradition he called upon a few trusted friends to form a "clearness committee" to help him with his decision. In this process the group, though refraining from giving advice, asks open, honest questions to help the seeker discover his or her own inner truth. For a while, the questions were easy: What is your vision for this institution? What is its mission in the larger society? How would you change the curriculum? How would you handle decision making? How would you deal with conflict?

Halfway into the process, someone asked a question that initially seemed easy, but turned out to be difficult, "What would you like most about being president?" It was the simplicity of the question that loosed him from his head and lowered him into his heart. Parker pondered the question for at least a full minute before he responded. Then, very softly and tentatively, he said, "Well, I would not like having to give up my writing and teaching. I would not like the politics of the presidency, never knowing who your real friends are. I would not like having to glad-hand people I do not respect simply because they have money. I would not like..."

Gently but firmly, the person who posed the question interrupted him, "May I remind you that I asked what you would most *like*?"

Parker responded impatiently, "Yes, yes, I'm working my way toward an answer." Then he resumed his litany, "I would not like having to give up my summer vacations. I would not like having to wear a suit and tie all the time. I would not like..."

Once again the questioner called him back to the original question. But this time Parker felt compelled to give the only honest answer he possessed, an answer that came from the very bottom of his barrel, an answer that appalled even him when he spoke it.

"Well," he said, in the smallest voice he possessed, "I guess what I'd like most is getting my picture in the paper with the word *president* under it."

These were seasoned Quakers who knew that though his answer was laughable, his mortal soul was at stake. They did not laugh at all but went into a long and serious silence. Finally, Parker's questioner broke the silence with a question that cracked everyone up and cracked Parker open. "Parker," he said, "can you think of an easier way to get your picture in the paper?"

Parker realized then that his desire to be president had much more to do with his ego than his ecology of life. He called the school and withdrew his name from consideration.[4]

The church, of course, is not infallible, which is why Paul instructed the church in Thessalonica to be discerning. He wrote,

> Do not quench the Spirit. Do not despise the words of the prophets, but test everything; hold fast to what is good; abstain from every form of evil." 1 Thess 5:19–22

There is no infallible word, either in sacred Scripture or in the Spirit-filled community. Paul admonished the church to be open to the voice of the Spirit as the Spirit speaks through the community, particularly

---

4. Palmer, *Let Your Life Speak*, 44–46.

through the voice of the prophets, but not to assume that everything spoken is God's will for the community. The community must exercise an ongoing process of discernment in light of the message and mission of Jesus Christ.

In the John 10 passage it is significant to note the emphasis on the power or authority given to Jesus to lay down his life for the sheep (John 10:17–18). While Jesus acted in unison with the Father, listening to his voice and obeying his will, he was not, however, an automaton. He was given the power to determine the course of his life, and he knew that if he continued on his present course he would continue to clash with the powers that be. His death, from this point of view, was inevitable, for the powers that be were determined to silence him. Jesus had the freedom to change paths, but he resolved, in love for the Father and in love for his disciples and the world, to continue the path that would inevitably lead to his death.

We, too, have been given the freedom to determine the course of our lives. We have the freedom to selfishly grasp for religious, political, and personal power. We, also, have the freedom to access the power of the Spirit, which is the power of love. We have the freedom to pursue positions of power and prominence, and we have the freedom to sacrificially lay down our lives in service for one another and our world.

According to John then, Jesus is the gate that leads to a flourishing life—a life of abundance (10:9–10). Entering through that gate leads to active involvement in God's project to transform the world, a transformation that begins in our own soul and body.

The image of a gate is also found in Matthew's Gospel. At the conclusion to the Sermon on the Mount, Jesus says,

> Enter through the narrow gate; for the gate is wide and the road is easy that leads to destruction, and there are many who take it. For the gate is narrow and the road is hard that leads to life, and there are few who find it. Matt 7:13

In Matthew's context, the gate represents the way of Jesus—the way of life he lived and taught his followers to live. The "narrow gate" is the way expounded in Jesus' teachings about how to live in God's kingdom.

How tragic that some versions of traditional Christianity make a particular kind of belief in Christ the gate that leads to life. As I have previously contended, there is nothing all that transforming in simply believing doctrines about Jesus (such as a belief regarding his divinity or a theory about the atonement). Unless there is clear intent to actually practice his teachings and pursue his path, a belief about Jesus is useless.

The gate that leads to a flourishing life is the gate that leads to discipleship. And discipleship is nothing short of apprenticeship; a relationship in which the disciple learns from Jesus Christ (the historic Jesus of Nazareth and the living, ever-present Christ) how to be authentically human and to live a flourishing life.

The image employed in John 4 to describe the flourishing life experienced in discipleship to Jesus is that of "a spring of water gushing up to eternal life" (4:14). In John 1:16, it refers to an inexhaustible reservoir of grace fed by eternal springs. The moment grace is drawn upon to replenish and renew the human condition, there is more than enough grace to take its place.

Disciples of Jesus are called to be channels and conduits of this grace, lavishing it upon the world in the same way it has been lavished upon them. A dynamic spiritual life involves both the inflow and outflow of the living water of the Spirit. The abundant life of the Spirit always moves disciples beyond their own interests and concerns into the wider world of need. This involves both conflict and engagement with the world.

OVERCOMING THE WORLD

In the Johannine literature, "world" has a wide range of meanings that are both negative and positive, and somewhat contradictory. On the positive side, the *Logos* (the Word) was instrumental in the creation of the world (John 1:10); the world is the inhabited world, the good creation of the good Creator. God loves the world (John 3:16) and sent Jesus into the world, not to judge the world, but to save it (John 12:47), to be the Savior of the world (1 John 4:12). He is the expiation (NRSV, "atoning sacrifice") for our sins, "and not for ours only but also for the sins of the whole world" (1 John 2:2). He is "the Lamb of God who takes away the sin of the world" (John 1:29, 36). God's plan, clearly, is to redeem the world.

On the negative side, the world can represent that which is under the power of evil and is opposed to God (John 7:7; 8:23; 1 John 2:15–17). The world is under the power of the evil one (1 John 5:19), who is the ruler of this world (John 12:31). Theologian and Bible scholar, Walter Wink has suggested that when "world" refers to "an alienating and alienated ethos" it is best translated as "System."[5] Wink described how many blacks struggling against apartheid in South Africa realized that freedom could not be gained by simply replacing the white leaders with blacks without changing the system. They named the evil and injustice that they were up against "The System." When police were at the door, those on the inside would warn, "The System is here." When they watched the evil propaganda on television they would quip, "The System is lying again." One of the ways they were able to get blacks to stop their collusion with the government was by saying to them, "You are supporting the System."

The writer of 1 John says this about the world (the System),

> Do not love the world or the things in the world. The love of the Father is not in those who love the world; for all that is in the world—the desire of the flesh, the desire of the eyes, the pride of riches—comes not from the Father but from the world. And the world and its desires are passing away, but those who do the will of God live forever. 1 John 2:15–17

The System is made up of systems: business, economic, religious, political, judicial, educational, and various other societal systems. These various systems interrelate and interconnect to form a cultural system. This text says that the world system, in its opposition to that which is of God, is permeated and pervaded by covetousness, greed, and selfish ambition. This does not mean, however, that the world system is totally corrupt. One of the distinct characteristics of Johannine theology is its sharply defined dualisms. Each component or category is accentuated by its opposite. Some major categories are: good/evil, light/darkness, love/hate, life/death, and Christ/the Devil. Real life, however, is not so clearly demarcated. Both good and evil are to be found within the systems of the world, though at this stage in our evolutionary development, many systems seem to be still tilted toward injustice.

All of us are socialized into world systems in various ways. Our family system plays an enormous role in this socialization process. We are all impacted and influenced by the forces of our culture, especially as these appeal to our ego desires in the process of becoming a separate

---

5. Wink, *Engaging the Powers*, 52.

"self." In systems where covetousness, greed, and selfish ambition exert a strong influence, the majority within that system tend to reflect these negative influences. Selfish and egotistical attitudes and prejudices can become deeply ingrained in our psyches. Of course, we are responsible for the persons we become, but "the principalities and powers" of the System have a major forming and shaping influence in our lives. The more that covetousness, greed, and selfish ambition pervade and control a system the more tilted toward evil it is and the more it takes on a life— a demonic spirituality—of its own.

In grappling with the dualisms of John's Gospel one must be careful, however, not to fall into a dualistic mode of thinking. God is at work in all aspects of society, ever piercing asunder our neat, clearly marked divisions of the sacred and the secular. Disciples of Jesus seek truth, justice, compassion, and the redemptive power of God's kingdom wherever they can find it. Disciples who live with open eyes and ready hearts can discern God's Spirit blowing in the most unusual places. Eruptions of God's new world into the present world can occur at any time and place, under all kinds of circumstances and conditions.

Evil and injustice in the organizations, systems, and institutions of the world may quench the Spirit. Greed and hate in our individual lives may grieve the Spirit. But the Spirit is still present, waiting for the opportunity to animate a conversation, inspire a speech, enliven a scene in a movie or a novel, evoke a feeling, recall an image, or implant a dream that will jar us awake to the light, warmth, and beauty of God's new world.

The biblical witness offers disciples of Jesus hope that they can overcome the System. The System may still beat them down and even kill them, but disciples do not have to be manipulated, controlled, and enslaved by it. When Jesus encountered the hostility of the religious leaders, he told them, "You are of this world, I am not of this world" (John 8:23). What he meant was, "You are living as if you belonged to the System; I live by the values of God's new world."

Jesus warned his disciples about persecution they would face in the System (John 15:18–20), and then he said, "But take courage; I have conquered the world!" (John 16:33) Jesus did not yield or conform to the System. He exposed the System. As the "light of the world" he illuminated the darkness and revealed the deception and deceit in the System. When mystics and prophets talk about seeing what is "Really

Real" they are talking about the capacity to see beyond the subtle deceptions, untruths, and crafty manipulations that the System uses to keep us in its grip.

Jesus overcame the System, and his followers can too (1 John 4:4). Jesus did not fight fire with fire. He did not return evil for evil. He did not overcome the System by using the System's methods of warfare. Jesus gave his life over to be crucified by the System in order to expose the hate and evil of the System, while simultaneously demonstrating God's love and intent to redeem the System. We, too, overcome as we follow the way of Jesus.

Jesus told Pilate, "My kingdom is not from this world. If my kingdom were from this world, my followers would be fighting to keep me from being handed over to the Jews. But as it is, my kingdom is not from here" (John 18:36). As I suggested earlier, Jesus is not saying that his kingdom is heavenly or other-worldly; he is saying that it does not partake of this worldly System. So his followers do not employ the methods of the System, such as violence. When Peter cuts off the ear of the servant of the high priest, trying to defend Jesus from arrest, Jesus tells him to put his sword away (John 18:11). It is his Father's will that he not respond violently and that he drink of the cup of suffering and death.

Jesus said "No" to the System, but God said "Yes" to Jesus, raising him from the dead, vindicating his life, message, and everything he stood for. In light of his approaching death Jesus tells his disciples,

> Very truly, I tell you, unless a grain of wheat falls into the earth and dies, it remains just a single grain; but if it dies, it bears much fruit. Those who love their life [in the System] lose it, and those who hate their life in this world [System] will keep it for eternal life. Whoever serves me must follow me, and where I am, there will my servant be also. Whoever serves me, the Father will honor. John 12:24–26

Overcoming the System involves dying to the System, dying to the covetousness, greed, and selfish ambition that inundates the System, dying to the lust for power, position, or possessions that keeps the System churning, dying to the need to control, manipulate, or deceive others, which are commonplace in the System. When we die to the lusts and passions that fuel the System, we are free to live by the passions and values of the kingdom of God.

The writer of 1 John declares, "This is the victory that overcomes the world, even our faith" (1 John 5:4). Faith is best understood here as faithfulness to Jesus' way of life. Never is faith, in John's Gospel or in the whole New Testament, simply to be equated with belief. Faith includes belief, but a dynamic, living Christian faith is expressed primarily through a commitment to the way of Jesus in the world.

Beliefs are important to the extent that beliefs determine how we live. We often do tend to live up or down to the actual beliefs we hold in the core of our being. Mother Teresa really did believe that she could see Jesus in the faces of the poor and dying in Calcutta. She believed that the service she rendered to the "least" of God's children (least from the world's point of view, not God's) she rendered to Jesus himself. Many suicide bombers genuinely believe that by dying for their militant cause they earn a place in Paradise. People do tend to live up or down to what is actually in their hearts. What matters about our beliefs are the ways in which our beliefs shape who we are and incite what we do.

How unfortunate today that so often Christian faith is erroneously reduced to what one intellectually believes. If you ask the average person on the street, or even the average Christian or church goer, what it means to have faith, that person is likely to recite a list of things that one must believe about Jesus. For many evangelical Christians the phrase "true believer" refers to someone who has, in their judgment, the right or correct beliefs about Christ. The faith that overcomes the world (the System), however, is the kind that engenders faithfulness to the way of Jesus in the world.

ENGAGING THE WORLD

Calvin Miller told about meeting a young Amish man named Reuben in Pennsylvania some years ago. Afterward, they began corresponding. Miller said, "It was the best correspondence I've ever had. Every letter was like hearing from the Apostle Paul. It was full of light and Scripture. I loved to hear from him and I always felt shallow when I answered him." One day Miller got a special letter. His friend wrote, "Sadie and I are getting married and we would like to come on our honeymoon and see you. Would that be okay?" Miller wrote back and told him to come.

They wore black clothes and they rode a bus. Miller's children looked at them like they were relics from the past. Miller took them to church and his church looked at them that way. Miller found himself living with people who had never listened to a radio or seen a television program or gone to a movie. He found himself explaining things. One of his kids had on a Dallas Cowboys sweatshirt. Reuben said, "I hear there are cowboys in the west." Miller said, "These aren't cowboys. These cowboys play football." He didn't understand. A world of definitions unfolded all week long.

On Thursday night, Calvin and his wife had season tickets to the Playhouse and were going to see Camelot. He asked Reuben and Sadie if they would like to go and they said they would. He tried to prepare them, "Now remember Reuben this is a play, and sometimes people do funny things in plays." Rueben said, "Calvin, I know your letters. You would never lead me into sin." Miller replied, "Sit down Reuben and let me tell you about the dirtiest parts of this play. Actors sometimes kiss each other on the mouth. Can you take that?" He thought he could. Miller said, "They wear leotards." He said, "What's leotards?" Miller tried to explain leotards, but this was difficult.

Thursday night arrived and Reuben and Sadie came out in the only clothes they had; all black. Miller's daughter whispered to him, "Dad, are they going to wear those clothes to the Playhouse?" He said, "Yeah." She said, "Can we go in after the lights go down?" He responded, "No, honey. These are our friends." Miller remarked, "All the way there I felt the tension between a man who wrote godly letters and what I was about to ask him to do."

So they watched Camelot. Every one there had seen Camelot except Reuben and Sadie. So Reuben and Sadie watched Camelot, and everyone else watched Reuben and Sadie watch Camelot.

When Reuben and Sadie went back to Pennsylvania, they wrote the Miller family a wonderful letter thanking them for everything, especially the play Camelot. Miller says, "You know something? I came to understand the person in tension with the Scriptures. I don't think Reuben understands. I think he loves God with all his heart, but he's completely unintelligible in a modern culture." Miller concluded, "You know what I think about true believers in Jesus? I think you might as well put on your black hat and black suit now. If we stand true to Jesus Christ in the world that's unfolding, we shall look as out of place to our culture as Reuben and Sadie looked to me."[6]

---

6. Miller, *PreachingToday* tape, 214.

I do not agree completely with Miller's conclusion, but there is no question that the values Jesus embodied and taught concerning God's new world are often diametrically at odds with the values of the world System. Disciples of Jesus do not belong to the System; they belong to God's new world. So how do disciples of Jesus engage the world?

It is essential for disciples of Jesus not to allow the System to name them and define them. In the story by C. S. Lewis, *The Lion, the Witch, and the Wardrobe*, Edmund, one of the four children who enter Narnia, joins the white witch. The white witch is the enemy of Aslan, the great lion, the King of Narnia and the Christ figure. Edmund betrays the others and falls under the power and control of the white witch. Aslan rescues Edmund, but then must give his own life to save Edmund from the witch's claim upon Edmund's life. Edmund has a change of heart and is sorry for what he has done.

After Edmund's rescue, the others see Aslan talking to Edmund alone. No one ever heard what Aslan said to Edmund, but it was a conversation that Edmund never forgot. As the others draw near, Aslan turns to meet them bringing Edmund with him. "Here is your brother," Aslan says, "and—there is no need to talk to him about what is past."

When the witch arrives, she requests a meeting with Aslan. The witch is familiar with the deep magic that the Emperor-beyond-the-Sea put into Narnia at the beginning, namely, that every traitor belongs to her. She says, "You have a traitor there Aslan." Everyone present knew that she meant Edmund. Lewis writes, "But Edmund had got past thinking about himself after all he'd been through and after the talk he had with Aslan that morning. He just went on looking at Aslan. It didn't seem to matter what the witch said."[7]

Edmund refused to allow the witch to claim him, name him, or define him. He kept his focus on Aslan and remembered the words Aslan had spoken. As disciples of Jesus, we do not listen to the negative accusations and descriptions of the world regarding who we are or what we are like. We do not belong to the System. We are God's children. As Jesus listened to the voice of the Father at his baptism by John—"This is my beloved Son, on whom my favor rests"—so disciples of Jesus listen to the voice of their loving, gracious Father/Mother who names them and claims them as his/her beloved daughters and sons.

---

7. Lewis, *The Chronicles of Narnia*, 174–75.

John 17 is commonly labeled by commentators as "Jesus' high priestly prayer," because the entire passage is a lengthy prayer of Jesus for his disciples. The prayer constitutes the final scene in Jesus' farewell discourse with his disciples, so even though it is framed as a prayer, it is primarily instructional. A portion of the prayer reads,

> I am asking on their behalf; I am not asking on behalf of the world, but on behalf of those whom you gave me, because they are yours. All mine are yours, and yours are mine; I have been glorified in them. And now I am no longer in the world, but they are in the world, and I am coming to you. Holy Father, protect them in your name that you have given me, so that they may be one, as we are one. While I was with them, I protected them in your name that you have given me . . . But now I am coming to you, and I speak these things in the world so that they may have my joy made complete in themselves. I have given them your word, and the world has hated them because they do not belong to the world, just as I do not belong to the world. I am not asking you to take them out of the world, but I ask you to protect them from the evil one. They do not belong to the world, just as I do not belong to the world. Sanctify them in the truth; your word is truth. As you have sent me into the world, so I have sent them into the world. And for their sakes I sanctify myself, so that they also may be sanctified in truth. John 17:9–19

In the above prayer, Jesus prayed that God would protect his followers from the cosmic powers that are opposed to the kingdom of God. He prayed that they would be one, even as he and his Father are one. As one, they will be able to resist the temptations and opposition of the world, while engaging the world as faithful representatives of the kingdom of God.

Being one cannot possibly mean that disciples will always be in agreement on matters of belief, theology, difficult social issues, or Christian practice. The "oneness" that Jesus is talking about must somehow relate to their loving one another the way Christ loved them. Christ loved them in spite of their misunderstandings and failures. He loved them, even when they denied him and deserted him (John 13:1). It is the enduring, steadfast, unconditional love of Christ that enables disciples to transcend all their differences in their care and compassion for one another, in their work for justice and peace, and in their service and ministry to the world.

Though the System at times will viciously attack the values embraced by disciples of Jesus, disciples need not withdraw or retreat in fear, nor compromise the values of God's kingdom. Like Jesus, they have consecrated themselves to be agents and representatives of God's kingdom in the world.

Jesus says, "Sanctify them in the truth; your word is truth. As you have sent me into the world, so I have sent them" (John 17:17-18). Sanctification, in this context, is related more to mission than morality. Johannine scholar, D. Moody Smith notes, "Their holiness, Jesus' and the disciples, is their being set apart from the world for the sake of the world."[8] To be set apart by the truth or word of God means, from John's perspective, to be set apart by Christ, who is the word (1:2, 12-14) and the truth (14:6). Those who share in Jesus' revelation of God and receive that revelation as the word and truth of God given to humanity, share also in the mission of Jesus to the world.

Some years ago, Tony Campolo initiated a program with Eastern College that trains people to go to Third World countries, as well as impoverished sections of American cities, with the express purpose of starting small businesses and cottage industries with the poor. This special MBA program was designed to help create employment for the poor, enabling them to escape from poverty.

Campolo, himself, was once part of a small business enterprise in the Dominican Republic. In an impoverished community in Santa Domingo, they started a small factory that produced sandals made out of worn-out automobile tires. With simple tools and minimal training, it was possible for young people to carve out the soles of sandals from discarded tires and make them into attractive and durable footwear. The boys sold them on the streets of the city, providing income for their families.

They told the younger children that if they would go out to the trash dumps and vacant lots of the city and bring them worn-out and discarded automobile tires, they would give them fifty-cents for each tire. It wasn't long before they had every old and discarded tire in Santa Domingo. Then they started bringing some new tires, and Campolo realized that they needed to make some adjustments.

Campolo says, "When we talk about Jesus, we make it clear that He is not just interested in our well-being in the afterlife. He is a Savior who

---

8. Smith, *John*, 316.

is at work in the world today trying to save the world from what it is, and make it into a place where people can live together with dignity."[9]

Discipleship to Jesus is not about believing the right things in order to escape the world; it's about doing the right things as part of God's plan to redeem the world. Disciples challenge the powers that be and work for justice in order to help extend God's peaceable kingdom.

Disciples of Jesus are also committed, like Jesus, to simple acts and deeds of compassion and mercy. While they do not lose the forest in the trees, they do not lose the trees in the forest. Disciples of Jesus live with a grand, glorious vision of a world transformed, while engaging in small, tangible acts of service and kindness.

Dr. Fred Craddock shared how his father used to complain about Sunday dinner being late when he and his mother came home from church. Sometimes the pastor would call, and his father would say, "I know what the church wants. The church doesn't care about me. The church wants another name, another pledge, another name, another pledge."

Sometimes they would have a revival. The pastor would bring the guest preacher to visit and "sic" him on his father. His father would say the same thing, "The church doesn't care about me; it just wants another name and another pledge." Fred must have heard it a thousand times.

The time came, however, when his father no longer made that accusation. He was in the veteran's hospital and weighed only seventy-three pounds. The Doctors had taken out his throat and said, "It's too late." They put in a metal tube, and X-rays burned him to pieces. Fred flew in to see him. He couldn't speak or eat. Fred looked around the room. There were potted plants and cut flowers on the windowsills, and a stack of cards twenty-inches deep beside his bed. Even the food tray had a flower on it. And all the flowers and cards were from the folks from the church—the very church of which his father use to say, "They don't care about me; they just want another name and another pledge."

Fred read one of the cards. His father couldn't speak, so his father took a Kleenex box and wrote on the side a line from Shakespeare. He wrote, "In this harsh world, draw your breath in pain to tell my story." Fred said, "What is your story, Daddy?" He wrote, "I was wrong."[10]

When the church is being the church, when disciples of Christ incarnate Christ's love through their actions and deeds, then the church

9. Campolo, *Let Me Tell You a Story*, 126.
10. Craddock, *Craddock Stories*, 14.

functions as the presence of Christ in the world. As the Father sent Christ, so has Christ sent his disciples to be coworkers with him by pursuing God's kingdom agenda of peace and justice, and by showering the world with acts and words of kindness and mercy.

In the Gospel of John, Jesus is identified as the Light of the world, the mediator of the abundant life of God (8:12). Disciples of Jesus engage and serve the world by reflecting, in whatever degree they are able, the light of the grace, goodness, love, compassion, and truth of God that is incarnate in Jesus.

According to writer Robert Fulghum, there is a Greek Orthodox monastery that sits on a rocky bay of the island of Crete, near the village of Gonia. Alongside it, on land donated by the monastery, sits an institute dedicated to peace and human understanding. Those who run the institute are particularly committed to rapprochement between Germans and Cretans. Fulghum writes,

> The site is important, because it overlooks the small airstrip at Maleme where Nazi paratroopers invaded Crete and were attacked by peasants wielding kitchen knives and hay scythes. The retribution was terrible. The populations of whole villages were lined up and shot for assaulting Hitler's finest troops. High above the institute is a cemetery with a single cross marking the mass grave of Cretan partisans. And across the bay on yet another hill is the regimented burial ground of the Nazi paratroopers.
>
> The memorials are so placed that all might see and never forget. Hate was the only weapon the Cretans had at the end, and it was a weapon many vowed never to give up. Never ever.
>
> Against this heavy curtain of history, in this place where the stone of hatred is hard and thick, the existence of an institute devoted to healing the wounds of war is a fragile paradox. How has it come to be here? The answer is a man. Alexander Papaderos.
>
> A doctor of philosophy, teacher, politician, resident of Athens but a son of this soil. At war's end he came to believe that the Germans and the Cretans had much to give one another—much to learn from one another. That they had an example to set. For if they could forgive each other and construct a creative relationship, then any people could.[11]

Fulghum attended a two week seminar at the institute on Greek culture led by experts recruited by Dr. Papaderos. At the end of the

---

11. Fulghum, *It Was on Fire When I Lay Down on It*, 172–73.

seminar, Papaderos invited final questions. The seminar, says Fulghum, had generated enough questions for a lifetime, but in the final moments there was only silence. Papaderos swept the room with his eyes. Fulghum couldn't resist. He asked, "Dr. Papaderos, what is the meaning of life?"

Laughter followed and the people stirred to go. But Papaderos held up his hand and stilled the room. He looked at Fulghum carefully to determine if he was serious. He could see that he was. Then he said, "I will answer your question." He took his wallet out of his pocket and brought out a very small mirror, about the size of a quarter. Then he said,

> When I was a small child, during the war, we were very poor and we lived in a remote village. One day, on the road, I found the broken pieces of a mirror. A German motorcycle had been wrecked in that place.
>
> I tried to find all the pieces and put them together, but it was not possible, so I kept only the largest piece. This one. And by scratching it on a stone I made it round. I began to play with it as a toy and became fascinated by the fact that I could reflect light into dark places where the sun would never shine—in deep holes and crevices and dark closets. It became a game for me to get light into the most inaccessible places I could find.
>
> I kept the little mirror, and as I went about my growing up, I would take it out in the idle moments and continue the challenge of the game. As I became a man, I grew to understand that this was not just a child's game but a metaphor for what I might do with my life. I came to understand that I am not the light or the source of light. But light—truth, understanding, knowledge—is there, and it will only shine in many dark places if I reflect it.
>
> I am a fragment of a mirror whose whole design and shape I do not know. Nevertheless, with what I have I can reflect light into the dark places of this world—into the black places in the hearts of men—and change some things in some people. Perhaps others may see and do likewise. This is what I am about. This is the meaning of life.[12]

In his prayer Jesus declares that he says these things so that his joy will be made complete in the disciples (17:13). Though disciples face opposition and hostility from the System in their engagement of the world, their lives are not marked by fear, anxiety, or drudgery. They share in the very joy of Christ.

---

12. Ibid., 174–75.

David McKenna, a former college and seminary president, tells about an experience he had at the start of his second college presidency. A distinguished scholar of American higher education visited their campus as a consultant on long-range planning. In their first meeting, he introduced himself as a "secular humanist." McKenna wondered how an avowed secular humanist might help create a vision for the future of an evangelical Christian university. His concluding statement changed McKenna's mind. After making all of his recommendations, he summarized his thoughts by saying, "I have been with you a week now. Frankly, I am still not sure what you mean by an 'evangelical Christian university.' But of this, I am sure. If you are what you say you are, this campus will be characterized by a note of joy."[13] It is interesting that one, who in no way claimed to be a disciple of Jesus, would so clearly connect joy with authentic Christian experience.

In the prayer Jesus says, "For them I sanctify myself, that they too may be truly sanctified" (17:19). Jesus voluntarily and intentionally set himself apart for God's work. God's purpose required Jesus' full cooperation and consecration to the mission. It was a creative partnership; it still is.

As disciples of Jesus, we too are called to sanctify ourselves, that is, to set ourselves apart to God's mission. We must choose to participate, collaborate, and be in creative partnership with Christ and God's dream for the world. As I have reiterated throughout this book, we have all been chosen, but we must decide to claim and live our calling as God's children. If the church is to have any impact and credibility in our contemporary age, it must stop trying to enforce its particular brand of Christianity on others and be about what Jesus was about—serving others and the creation, as well as confronting the powers that be through love. And this involves a willingness to endure suffering and share in the suffering of others.

SUFFERING LOVE

At the beginning of Hebrews 12, immediately following an exposition on faith and a litany of praise to faithful believers of the past (Heb 11), the writer exhorts his readers,

---

13. McKenna, *Mark*, 68.

> Therefore, since we are surrounded by so great a cloud of witnesses, let us also lay aside every weight and the sin that clings so closely, and let us run with perseverance the race that is set before us, looking to Jesus the pioneer and perfecter of our faith, who for the sake of the joy that was set before him endured the cross, disregarding its shame, and has taken his seat at the right hand of the throne of God.
>
> Consider him who endured such hostility against himself from sinners, so that you may not grow weary or lose heart. In your struggle against sin you have not yet resisted to the point of shedding your blood....
>
> Therefore lift your dropping hands and strengthen your weak knees, and make straight paths for your feet, so that what is lame may not be put out of joint, but rather be healed. Heb 12:1–4, 12–13

The Letter to the Hebrews is a very unusual document. Although it concludes with greetings the way a letter would conclude, there is no opening greeting and no identification of the writer or recipients. The author calls this document a "word of exhortation" (13:22), a phrase that is used by Luke to describe a synagogue sermon (Acts 13:15). The author, steeped in Judaism, utilizes a highly elaborate rhetorical strategy that alternates between argument and exhortation, and he applies allegorical and typological interpretations of the Hebrew Scriptures to Christ. The writer must also have been immersed in the Greek world, since his arguments and interpretations rely heavily upon Greek philosophical categories and ideas. He expected this congregation to think deeply about their faith and to grasp some highly developed theological arguments.

The basic pastoral situation can be deduced from the document itself. The author seems to be addressing an urgent problem that was threatening to divide and diminish the witness of this congregation. Disciples were leaving the church, not, however, to go to another church. Homiletics and Bible scholar, Thomas Long observed, "The threat to this congregation is not that they are charging off in the wrong direction; they do not have enough energy to charge anywhere."[14] They were dropping out of the race, forsaking their faith, and yielding to the pressure of the System. Tired of walking the walk, they were walking away from the Christian community.

14. Long, *Hebrews*, 3.

The author employs imagery from the world of athletics. Discipleship to Jesus is compared to running a race. The Greek word that is translated "race" (*agon*) is a word from which we get the word "agonize." Runners who train to be competitive agonize through the hardships and challenges of intense physical conditioning. They lay aside every encumbrance, weight, and hindrance, and train with rigorous self-discipline. They give their lives to it, knowing full well that emotional and physical struggle are part of the journey.

With equal determination, disciples of Jesus pursue God's dream for the world in collaboration with the living Christ and with all who are committed to building families, communities, and societies pervaded by goodness, justice, forgiveness, and grace. It is a worthy cause. There is no insignificant task. There are no lesser or greater members within God's family, regardless of belief or religious affiliation (or lack thereof). All are called and chosen for important work.

Disciples of Jesus are singularly focused. As athletes give themselves completely to the pursuit of their dream, so do disciples of Jesus. In the movie, *City Slickers*, Billy Crystal plays Mitch Robbins, who is going through a midlife crisis. He is torn between his desire to advance his career and his obligation to his family. His life is scattered and divided. The lives of his two best friends are also in crisis. Phil is trapped managing his father-in-law's grocery store, while stuck in a loveless marriage. Ed, a successful business man and former playboy, is struggling with the commitment required in a monogamous marriage and with the pressure to have a child. At Mitch's thirty-ninth birthday party his two friends present their gift: a two-week cattle drive that all three men will participate in.

Jack Palance plays Curly, the tough-as-nails, wise-to-the-ways-of-the-world, trail boss. He is aware of the crisis in meaning that the three men are having. In a wonderful scene Curly asks Mitch if he would like to know the meaning of life. He hold's up one finger and says, "It's this." Mitch responds, "The secret of life is your finger?" Curly, never batting an eye, says, "It's one thing. The secret of life is pursuing one thing." He can't tell Mitch what that is; he will have to discover that for himself.[15]

The singular commitment and passion of Jesus to do God's will and to see God's new world realized serve as the catalyst for Christ's followers. Jesus is the "pioneer and perfecter of our faith." He blazes the trail

---

15. *City Slickers*, Columbia Pictures, 1991.

and opens the path before us. He is our model and example of a race run well.

Our lives tend to be cluttered and divided. We feel the strain of many obligations. Thomas Kelly, the Quaker educator, scholar, and writer, expressed elegantly our condition in his spiritual classic, *A Testament of Devotion*,

> The outer distractions of our interests reflect an inner lack of integration of our own lives. We are trying to be several selves at once, without all our selves being organized by a single, mastering Life within us. Each of us tends to be, not a single self, but a whole committee of selves. There is the civic self, the parental self, the financial self, the religious self, the society self, the professional self, the literary self. And each of our selves is in turn a rank individualist, not co-operative but shouting out his vote loudly for himself when the voting time comes. And all too commonly we follow the common American method of getting a quick decision among conflicting claims within us. . . . We feel honestly the pull of many obligations and try to fulfill them all.[16]

Kelly argued that the solution to this divided condition is learning how to live out of the divine center, the living Christ, the "beyond that is within," and to look out upon the world through the lens of this divine light. He wrote, "Life is meant to be lived from a Center, a divine Center. Each one of us can live such a life of amazing power and peace and serenity, of integration and confidence and simplified multiplicity, on one condition—that is, if we really want to."[17]

As we live from the Center and invest our lives in the kingdom of God, the Love that sends us out into the world to spend ourselves in ministry gives us power, peace, and joy in the fulfillment of our calling. This is because God portions out God's vast concern in bundles and gives to each one of us our portion. This becomes our task. We do not have to save the world.

There is joy in service, in struggle, in giving our lives to the "one thing." The writer of Hebrews says, "[Jesus] for the sake of the joy that was set before him endured the cross, disregarding its shame, and has taken his seat at the right hand of the throne of God" (12:2). The reference to Jesus' current position is actually a statement regarding God's vindication of his life and death. He lived for God and took his rightful

16. Kelly, *A Testament of Devotion*, 91–92.
17. Ibid., 93.

place with God, even though it meant a cruel, humiliating execution on a cross. The race run for God's cause in the world is marked by discipline, struggle, suffering, and hardship, and is, paradoxically, the way to true and lasting joy. Those given to self-fulfillment find joy elusive. Those given to the "one thing" (the kingdom of God) experience joy, even when the tables are turned against them and they know they are going to lose. The winning is in the enduring, persevering against all opposition, being faithful to what is good, true, just, and right.

Disciples who keep their focus on Jesus as the trailblazer for their own faith and life will experience a peace and joy deeper than their grief and pain. They know suffering, but suffering doesn't define them or hold them back. Disciples of Jesus are sustained by the courage, strength, and joy of God's Spirit.

Jesus sets the pattern for a life well lived, a life lived out of the divine center. When the love of God fills us, the blinders fall from our eyes and we are enabled to see all people in a new way. As Jesus offered his life in service through the Spirit, even unto death, so the Spirit leads us to suffer with our brothers and sisters who are hurting. Jesus, in his life and especially in his death, took on the suffering, pain, and evil of the human condition. To follow Christ is to join Christ in his solidarity with the human plight.

The goal of the life of discipleship, however, is not suffering; rather, suffering is the inevitable consequence of a life well lived. The liberating joy of the disciple is that the disciple, focused on the kingdom of God, is no longer bound by selfish ambition, greed, and the need for recognition. The disciple is free to take up his or her cross and follow Jesus into solidarity and union with our suffering world. Suffering, then, can be welcomed as a companion along with joy, as we journey with Christ to serve others and enhance life on this planet. Theologian and Scripture scholar, Douglas John Hall reminds us that the church's suffering is perennial and manifold. He has written, "If the church does not see this suffering and if, seeing it, does not take the burden of it upon itself, then its whole life must be called into question."[18] Pursuing the path of Jesus in the power of his Spirit leads disciples to not only bear their own suffering with endurance and courage, but to bear also the sufferings of others.

---

18. Hall, *The Cross in Our Context*, 152–53.

Cormac McCarthy's, *The Road*, was awarded the Pulitzer Prize for fiction in 2007. It is a story about a journey taken by a father and his young son during a period of several months, over a ruined, ravaged landscape, which was the result of some unexplained cataclysmic (the hints suggest nuclear) destruction of the world. The sun is obscured by dark clouds and all plant life has been extinguished. What is left of humanity consists mostly of roving bands of cannibals and refugees who scavenge for food. The father's mission is to keep the son alive, so as "to carry the fire." He tells his son that he is appointed by God to keep him alive and will kill anyone who touches him. This mission causes the father to avoid anything that would jeopardize his son's life, refusing even to give some of their food and clothing to others who will die without them.

His son is characterized by a kind of innocent goodness. It pierces his heart when his father refuses to help the stragglers they run across on their journey. His father knows that what little they have they desperately need to survive. In this demonic world where the fear of surviving is just as great as the fear of dying, the son is a marvel. The boy knows terror, but not hate. He struggles with the ambiguity of "carrying the fire" and being "the good guys," while his father denies assistance or help to the dying. On one occasion he asks his father, "Are we still the good guys?"

In one scene, the father and son have all their goods stolen by a single thief. They are able to determine his direction and overtake him. The thief has a knife, but the father has a gun (with a single bullet, though the thief doesn't know that). The father recaptures all their goods and then demands that the thief completely strip. The boy protests. Here is part of the interchange,

> The thief looked at the boy. The boy had turned away and put his hands over his ears. Okay, he said. Okay. He sat naked in the road and began to unlace the rotting pieces of leather laced to his feet. Then he stood up, holding them in one hand.
> Put them in the cart. [The father is speaking]
> He stepped forward and placed the shoes on top of the blankets and stepped back. Standing there raw and naked, filthy, starving. Covering himself with his hand. He was already shivering.
> Put the clothes in.
> He bent and scooped up the rags in his arms and piled them on top of the shoes. He stood there holding himself. Don't do this man.
> You didn't mind doing it to us.
> I'm begging you.

> Papa, the boy said.
> Come on. Listen to the kid.
> You tried to kill us.
> I'm starving, man. You'd have done the same.
> You took everything.
> Come on, man. I'll die.
> I'm going to leave you the way you left us.
> Come on. I'm begging you.
> He pulled the cart back and swung it around and put the pistol on top and looked at the boy. Let's go, he said. And they set out along the road south with the boy crying and looking back at the nude and slatlike creature standing there in the road shivering and hugging himself. Oh, Papa, he sobbed.
> Stop it.
> I can't stop it.
> What do you think would have happened to us if we hadn't caught him? Just stop it.
> I'm trying.

The boy could not stop crying and finally just sat down in the road sobbing. The father walked back up the road, but couldn't see the thief. He tells the boy that he is gone, but his son insists that he is not.

> What do you want to do?
> Just help him, Papa. Just help him.
> The man looked back up the road.
> He was just hungry, Papa. He's going to die.
> He's going to die anyway.
> He's so scared, Papa.
> The man squatted and looked at him. I'm scared, he said. Do you understand? I'm scared.
> The boy didn't answer. He just sat there with his head bowed, sobbing.
> You're not the one who has to worry about everything.
> The boy said something but he couldn't understand him. What? he said. He looked up, his wet and grimy face. Yes I am, he said. I am the one.[19]

The son says, "Yes, I am the one." The son is the one who has to bear the suffering of the world. I have no idea what McCarthy's original intent was in the passage above, but I interpret it as an echo of the compassion of the Son and his followers, who are called to solidarity with our suffering planet.

19. McCarthy, *The Road*, 257–59.

When the writer of Hebrews instructs his readers to look to Jesus and consider how he endured the shame, hostility, and suffering of the cross, he is telling them to run the same race, to join Jesus in his suffering love for the world. Part of what it means to take up our cross and follow Jesus is to share his heart and compassion, to bear in suffering love the depth of the world's evil, along with the alienation and brokenness that are its consequences. In the beautiful words of Thomas Kelly, when we live out of the divine center of God's love as Jesus did, then there "is a sense in which, in this terrible tenderness, we become one with God and bear in our quivering souls the sins and burdens, the benightedness and the tragedy of the creatures of the whole world, and suffer in their suffering, and die in their death."[20]

Suffering is a natural consequence of the life of discipleship. When Jesus told his disciples to take up their cross and follow him, he made suffering part of the package. The cross, of course, has symbolic connotations, expressing the necessity of dying to the ego. But this existential meaning is not its singular meaning, nor does it eliminate its connection to actual suffering.

Suffering, as we all know, is not unique to disciples of Jesus. It is part of the common lot of humanity, but disciples of Jesus intentionally enter into the suffering of others and our planet. One paradox of the spiritual life is that suffering forms the crucible in which disciples experience the transformative power of God. In writing to the Philippians, Paul expressed his desire to share in the sufferings of Christ so that he might experience the transforming power of Christ's resurrection (Phil 3:10–11).

Discipleship to Jesus enables us to draw upon Christ's joy and strength when we face opposition and when the Spirit leads us to identify with others in their suffering. Christ blazes the trail before us. Alexander Solzhenitsyn has shared of the time he was in the Russian Gulag when he despaired of life. His life in prison consisted of constant shoveling. One day he laid down his shovel and sat down on a little make-shift bench with his head between his knees. He had watched guards beat prisoners to death who quit shoveling. He felt someone come over next to him and he braced himself for the pain. But it was an elderly man, a fellow prisoner. The man reached down and picked up a twig, and drew in the

---

20. Kelly, *A Testament of Devotion*, 81.

dirt, in front of Solzhenitsyn, the sign of the cross. Then Solzhenitsyn understood and he got up and shoveled.

There is joy and fullness of life in discipleship to Jesus. There is also hardship and suffering. When the pressures, struggles, and temptations to quit are most intense, we must keep our focus on Jesus so that we will not lose heart and give in to our weariness. It is Christ who gives us the strength to lift up our drooping hands and weak knees. Christ supports and empowers us in our suffering, often healing what is lame, mending what is broken, restoring balance to our lives and our communities, so that we may know and share with our world God's love and grace, and the vision of a world made right.

Bibliography

Abernethy, Bob, and William Bole. *The Life of Meaning: Reflections on Faith, Doubt, and Repairing the World*. With a foreword by Tom Brokaw. New York: Seven Stories, 2007.
Anspaugh, David, director. *Hoosiers*. DVD. Written by Angelo Pizzo. Hemdale Film Corporation, 1986.
Barr, Nevada. *Seeking Enlightenment Hat by Hat: A Skeptics Path to Religion*. New York: Berkley, 2003.
Barrett, C. K. *The Epistle to the Romans*. Harper's New Testament Commentaries. New York: Harper & Row, 1957.
Bonhoeffer, Dietrich. *The Cost of Discipleship*. New York: Touchstone, 1995.
Borg, Marcus J. *Jesus: Uncovering the Life, Teachings, and Relevance of a Religious Revolutionary*. New York: HarperSanFrancisco, 2006.
———. *Reading the Bible Again for the First Time: Taking the Bible Seriously but Not Literally*. New York: HarperSanFrancisco, 2001.
———. *The Heart of Christianity: Rediscovering a Life of Faith*. New York: HarperSanFrancisco, 2003.
Borg, Marcus J., and N. T. Wright. *The Meaning of Jesus: Two Visions*. New York: HarperSanFrancisco, 1999.
Boring, M. Eugene. *The Gospel of Matthew: Introduction, Commentary, and Reflections*. The New Interpreter's Bible, Vol. VIII. Nashville: Abingdon, 1995.
Brooks, James L., director. *As Good as it Gets*. DVD. Written by Mark Andrus and James L. Brooks. Columbia Tristar Pictures, 1997.
Brown, Raymond E. *The Gospel According to John, I-XII: Introduction, Translation, and Notes*. The Anchor Bible, 29A. New York: Doubleday, 1966.
———. *The Gospel According to John, XIII-XXI: Introduction, Translation, and Notes*. The Anchor Bible, 29A. New York: Doubleday, 1970.
Bruce, F. F. *The Epistle to the Galatians: A Commentary on the Greek Text*. The New International Greek Testament Commentary. Grand Rapids, Mich.: Eerdmans, 1982.
Campolo, Tony. *Let Me Tell You a Story: Life Lessons from Unexpected Places and Unlikely People*. W. Publishing Group, 2000.
Coffin, William Sloan. *A Passion for the Possible: A Message to U.S. Churches*, 2nd ed. With a foreword by Martin E. Marty. Louisville: Westminster, 2004.
———. *Credo*. With a forward by James Carroll. Louisville: Westminster, 2004.
———. *Letters to a Young Doubter*. Louisville: Westminster, 2005.
Craddock, Fred B. *Craddock Stories*. Edited by Mike Graves and Richard F. Ward. St. Louis: Chalice, 2001.
Crossan, John Dominic. *God and Empire: Jesus Against Rome, Then and Now*. New York: HarperOne, 2007.

Culpepper, R. Alan. *The Gospel of Luke: Introduction, Commentary, and Reflections.* The New Interpreter's Bible, Vol. IX. Nashville, Abingdon, 1995.

Dawn, Maggie. "Faith Matters: Second Thoughts." *The Christian Century* (March 11, 2008) 37.

Dunn, James D. *Jesus' Call to Discipleship.* Understanding Jesus Today. Cambridge: Cambridge University Press, 1992.

Dunnam, Maxie D. *Exodus.* The Communicator's Commentary Series, Old Testament, Vol. 2. Word, Inc., 1987.

Epperly, Bruce G. *Holy Adventure: 41 Days of Audacious Living.* Nashville: Upper Room, 2008.

Fulghum, Robert. *It Was on Fire When I Lay Down on It.* New York: Ivy Books, 1988.

Gomes, Peter. *The Scandalous Gospel of Jesus: What's So Good About the Good News?* New York: HarperOne, 2007.

Hall, John Douglas. *The Cross in Our Context: Jesus and the Suffering World.* Minneapolis: Fortress, 2003.

Hays, Richard B. *First Corinthians.* Interpretation: A Bible Commentary for Teaching and Preaching. Louisville: John Knox, 1997.

Jackson, Mick, director. *Tuesdays with Morrie.* DVD. Produced by Oprah Winfrey and Kate Forte. Touchstone, 1999.

Jewison, Norman, director. *The Hurricane.* DVD. Written by Armyan Bernstein and Dan Gordon. Universal Pictures, 1999.

Jordan, Clarence. *The Substance of Faith: And Other Cotton Patch Sermons.* Edited by Dallas Lee. With a foreword by Jimmy Carter. Eugene, OR: Cascade, 2005.

Kelly, Thomas. *A Testament of Devotion.* With an introduction by Richard Foster. New York: HarperSanFrancisco, 1941.

Kraybill, Donald B. *The Upside-Down Kingdom.* 25th anniversary ed. Scottdale, Pennsylvania: Herald, 3003.

Larson, Bruce. *Luke.* The Communicators Commentary, Vol. 3. Waco: Word, 1983.

Lauback, Frank C. *Frank Laubach: Man of Prayer.* Laubach Literacy International, 1990. Quoted in John Ortburg, *If You Want to Walk on Water, You've Got to Get Out of the Boat,* 164. Grand Rapids: Zondervan, 2001.

Lewis, C. S. "The Lion, the Witch, and the Wardrobe." In *The Chronicles of Narnia,* First American ed. New York: HarperCollins, 2001.

Lightner, Robert P. *Evangelical Theology: A Survey and Review.* Grand Rapids, MI: Baker, 1986.

Long, Thomas G. *Hebrews.* Interpretation: A Biblical Commentary for Teaching and Preaching. Louisville: John Knox, 1997.

———. "Sermon: Once I Was Blind, But Now . . . ?" In *Preaching John's Gospel: The World it Imagines,* edited by David Fleer and Dave Bland. St. Louis: Chalice, 2008.

Marsh, Charles. *Wayward Christian Soldiers: Freeing the Gospel from Political Captivity.* Oxford: Oxford University Press, 2007.

McCarthy, Cormac. *The Road.* New York: Vintage, 2006.

McKenna, David L. *Mark.* The Communicators Commentary, Vol. 2. Waco: Word Books, 1982.

Miller, Calvin. *Into the Depths of God: Where Eyes See the Invisible, Ears Hear the Inaudible, and Minds Conceive the Inconceivable.* Minneapolis: Bethany House, 2000.

Nichols, Mike, director. *Wit.* DVD. Written by Emma Thompson and Mike Nichols. HBO films, 2001.

Nouwen, Henry J. M. *Making All Things New: An Invitation to the Spiritual Life*. New York: HarperSanFrancisco, 1981.
Ortburg, John. *If You Want to Walk on Water, You've Got to Get Out of the Boat*. Grand Rapids: Zondervan, 2001.
Palmer, Parker J. *A Hidden Wholeness: The Journey Toward An Undivided Life*. San Francisco: Jossey-Bass, 2004.
———. *Let Your Life Speak: Listening for the Voice of Vocation*. San Francisco: Jossey-Bass, 2000.
Peterson, Eugene. *Leap Over a Wall: Earthly Spirituality for Everyday Christians*. New York: HarperSanFrancisco, 1997.
Pregeant, Russell. *Engaging the New Testament: An Interdisciplinary Introduction*. Minneapolis: Fortress, 1995.
Queen, Chuck. *The Good News According to Jesus: A New Kind of Christianity for a New Kind of Christian*. Macon, Georgia: Smyth and Helwys, 2009.
Ratner, Brett, director. *The Family Man*. DVD. Written by David Diamond and David Weissman. Universal Pictures, 2000.
Rohr, Richard. *Everything Belongs: The Gift of Contemplative Prayer*. Revised ed. New York: Crossroad, 2003.
———. *Hope Against Darkness: The Transforming Vision of Saint Francis in an Age of Anxiety*. Cincinnati: St Anthony Messenger Press, 2001.
Rollins, Peter. *How (Not) to Speak of God*. Brewster, Mass: Paraclete, 2006.
Salzberg, Sharon. *Faith: Trusting Your Own Deepest Experience*. New York: Riverhead Books, 2002.
Sanguin, Bruce. "Paying Homage: Being Christian in a World of Many Faiths." In *The Emerging Christian Way: Thoughts, Stories, and Wisdom for a Faith Transformation*, edited by Michael Schwartzentruber. Canada: CopperHouse, 2006.
Schweizer, Eduard. *The Good News According to Matthew*. Translated by David E. Green. Atlanta: John Knox, 1975.
Selmanovic, Samir. *It's Really All About God: Reflections of a Muslim Athiest Jewish Christian*. San Francisco: Jossey-Bass, 2009.
Smith, D. Moody. *John*. Abingdon New Testament Commentaries. Nashville: Abingdon, 1999.
Speilberg, Steven, director. *Artificial Intelligence: A. I.* DVD. Screen story written by Ian Watson. Warner Brothers, 2001.
Steindl-Rast, Brother David. *Gratefulness, the Heart of Prayer: An Approach to Life in Fullness*. New York/Mahwah, N.J.: Paulist, 1984.
Storper, Craig, director. *Open Range*. DVD. Written by Lauran Paine. Touchstone Pictures, 2003.
Tewell, Thomas. "Don't Put a Period Where God Puts a Coma." Preaching Today, cassette tape #247.
Tickle, Phyllis. *The Great Emergence: How Christianity is Changing and Why*. Grand Rapids, MI: Baker, 2008.
Underwood, Ron, director. *City Slickers*. DVD. Written by Lowell Ganz and Babaloo Mandel. Columbia Pictures, 1991.
Weir, Peter, director. *The Truman Show*. DVD. Produced by Andrew Niccol, Scott Rudin, and Adam Schroeder. Paramount Pictures, 1998.
Willard, Dallas. *The Divine Conspiracy: Rediscovering Our Hidden Life in God*. New York: HarperSanFrancisco, 1998.

Willimon, William H. *Thank God It's Friday: Encountering the Seven Last Words from the Cross*. With a foreword by Marva Dawn. Nashville: Abingdon, 2006.

Wills, Gary. *What Paul Meant*. New York: Viking, 2006.

Wink, Walter. *Engaging the Powers: Discernment and Resistance in a World of Domination*. Minneapolis: Fortress, 1992.

———. *The Powers That Be: Theology for a New Millennium*. New York: Galilee/Doubleday, 1998.

Wolpe, David J. *Why Faith Matters*. With a foreword by Rick Warren. New York: HarperOne, 2008.

Wright, N. T. *Surprised by Hope: Rethinking Heaven, the Resurrection, and the Mission of the Church*. New York: HarperOne, 2008.

Ziesler, John. *Pauline Christianity*. Revised ed. Oxford Bible Series, gen. eds. R. R Ackroyd and G. N. Stanton. Oxford: Oxford University Press, 1990.

www.ingramcontent.com/pod-product-compliance
Lightning Source LLC
Chambersburg PA
CBHW060820190426
43197CB00038B/2164